Author of Crime, Criminals, & Redemption

POLICING
IN FAITH

**A Discussion About The Police,
For The Police, and
The People They Serve**

STACI SWEET
Contributor - Christian A. Sweet

Unless otherwise indicated, all Scripture quotations are taken from the New King James Version Bible®. Copyright © 1982 by Thomas Nelson. Used by permission. All rights reserved. Copyright © 2011 by Common English Bible. Amplified Bible, Classic Edition **(AMPC)** Copyright © 1954, 1958, 1962, 1964, 1965, 1987 by The Lockman Foundation. New Life Version **(NLV)** Copyright © 1969, 2003 by Barbour Publishing, Inc.; Easy-to-Read Version **(ERV)** Copyright © 2006 by Bible League International; Any definitions, unless otherwise stated, are taken from the New Strong's Exhaustive Concordance with some emphasis added by the Author.

Cover designed by Staci Sweet

Policing In Faith: A Discussion About The Police, For The Police, And The People They Serve

ISBN: 979-8-218-15108-9

Copyright © 2022

All rights reserved. No part of this book may be reproduced, stored in retrieval system, or transmitted by any means – electronic, mechanical, photographic (photocopying), recording, or otherwise – without prior permission in writing from the author – unless the author's blurb, sole credit and/or contact information is attached. For more information, contact realissuespublishing@gmail.com.

Author and Publisher claim no responsibility for any person or entity for any liability, loss, or damage caused or alleged to be caused directly or indirectly as a result of the use, application or interpretation of book material.

Staci Sweet is not affiliated, endorsed by or sponsored by any law enforcement agency.

Printed in USA
Faithables®, LLC. d/b/a Real Issues Publishing
Dallas, TX 75228

Table of Contents

Preface

Chapter 1: **Positively Identifying the Son of God** 13

Chapter 2: **Officer Suicides** 19

Chapter 3: **Civilian Complaint Process** 25

Chapter 4: **The Code of Silence** 29

Chapter 5: **Correction Byway of Repentance** 41

Chapter 6: **Objective Reasoning** 63

Chapter 7: **Lawful Orders, Probable Cause & Use of Force** 79

Chapter 8: **The Objective Reasonableness Behind Fearful Use of Force** 99

Chapter 9: **What's Love Got To Do ... With Law Enforcement** 113

Chapter 10: **Use-of-Force Incidences in the Bible** 147

Chapter 11: **Good Cops** 151

Chapter 12: **Psychological Evaluations** 159

Chapter 13: **The Defund the Police Movement** 165

Chapter 14: **Evasions and Escapes** 169

Protection & Policing Confessions for Law Enforcement

Systemic Change Prayers and Confessions for We, the People

Appendix

...**to my extraordinary son, Christian**...

You saved my life before you were born and have continued to do so in more ways than you'll ever know. You were created to protect, and I am so thankful God saw fit to give you a gift that's not just for me but for the nations. Though every door into law enforcement has been locked, this book holds the key.

Preface

It was Monday, October 13, 2014, when I saw an Instagram post of Dr. Cornell West, former Professor of the Practice of Public Philosophy at Harvard University and Professor Emeritus at Princeton University and Dr. Jamal Bryant, social justice advocate and Senior Pastor of New Birth Missionary Baptist Church, being arrested for demanding that the Ferguson Police Department be held accountable for the wrongful death of Michael Brown, a young 18-year-old Black man fatally shot by Darren Wilson, a Ferguson police officer who'd been on the force three years prior to the shooting. When I saw that he, and other men of God, had been taken into custody, it grieved me to the point that I woke up in the middle of the night to pray and ask God if there were accounts of police brutality in scripture that I could study to get some guidance and biblical clarity on the subject because to most, the state of policing today seems hopeless. But because I am a student of the Word, I knew that if I could find at least two witnesses of biblical precedence to stand on, then we, meaning the people, could not only have hope but could bring a solution to this mounting issue. Much to my surprise, He led me to what has become the book you are reading now, **Policing in Faith: A Discussion About The Police, For The Police, and The People They Serve.**

As I began to study the scriptures, I soon discovered that instead of this book being a one-sided us-against-the-police type of work, it would be an all-inclusive body of work which would house hope, instruction, and biblical precedence of interactions between we the people, while also providing guidance for law enforcement of how the Bible says officers should conduct themselves. I must admit, it took well over five years for the Lord to convince me to write the book. Not that I am an overly disobedient child of the Most High, but my disdain for law enforcement was at an all-time high. In fact, I questioned if what I was hearing in my heart was even the spirit of the Lord. But over the years I've discovered that God has always '…**chosen the foolish things of the world to put to shame the wise**…' (1 Corinthians 1:27) Therefore, it is His modus operandi to choose someone who has an extreme aversion for a person, thing, or cause in order to change his or her way of thinking while simultaneously bringing the truth of His perspective to light. By doing so, that once adversarial person can provide a 360° view on the subject so as to leave no room for doubt or debate by advocates and critics alike. One such person was Paul the Apostle who admitted to punishing, incarcerating and persecuting, Christians. Yet God chose him to write three-fourths of the New Testament, and though he did, he even questioned his qualifications. The same is true for me because I did not take this assignment willingly. Not only did I not want to author this book, but I am highly unqualified.

I have neither a background in law enforcement nor do I hold any type of criminal justice degree. Yet God chose me. Not because I'm qualified but because I was available. I know with certainty that there were several high-ranking, long tenured officers, nationwide, chosen for this assignment but turned it down. God chose me simply because I prayed a prayer, told Him yes, and sought the solution in His Word. That said, if you are still questioning my credentials, I encourage you to refer to the scriptures where God used one shepherd to kill a military superpower; a queen to expose an existential threat, and a Man born of a virgin to not only die for all mankind but to go to the regions of hell and defeat God's archenemy in three days. So, think it not strange for God to use the least likely to bring about change in the culture of policing.

Change is going to happen the same way it always has…byway of prayer. David prayed. Esther prayed, and Jesus prayed but that's not all they did, and neither should we. But because we do, God will give some of us the plans and policies needed while placing others of us in positions of power to ensure that those who abuse their policing authority are held accountable. But first, we must locate instances of proper policing, in the scriptures as well as locate examples of how communities should be policed in addition to locating incidents of police violence – in the Word. Once we, **as believers**, investigate these instances, then we, **the people**, will then be in a better position to align our faith and prayers in accordance with the Word so that we, the people can become members of law enforcement; so that we, the people, can do the work needed to ensure that God-ordained decision makers have the wisdom and votes needed to pass legislation to make a change and so that we, the people, can receive the wisdom, strategy, and favor needed to reposition ourselves to become those decision makers.

> "What does it profit, my brethren, if someone says he has faith but does not have works? Can faith save him? [15] If a brother or sister is [being brutalized by police], [16] and one of you says to them, "[I wish someone would do something about it]," but you do not [vote and do the things necessary to make a change], what does it profit? [17] Thus also faith by itself, if it does not have works, is dead. [18] But someone will say, "You have faith, and I have works." Show me your faith without your works, and I will show you my faith by my works."
>
> – James 2:14-18 NKJV
> (*Author paraphrase for emphasis*)

If you're still reading, then it's possible that you're either an intercessor which means you've been called to pray about the state of policing today or you're being groomed to become a decision maker or a member of law enforcement. You've either been doing the work of an activist or you're now being prepared to do the spiritual legwork required to navigate, legislate, and govern in your given space, or even better – you're already a believer currently working in law enforcement. In which case, you should read this book with the intent of learning how to properly police in accordance with the scriptures. On the other hand, you could be an unbelieving skeptic looking to find fault and/or prove me wrong. If that's you, then I can tell you upfront, that even you'll walk away referring to something mentioned in this book. Either way, we all have a part to play. So, to you I say get in position and get ready because it's time for us to do the spiritual investigative work needed in order to effect change. That being said, let's get to the first order of business which is to see what the Bible says about policing.

Please note: Throughout the book, you'll come across Sweet Solutions. Sweet Solutions is my attempt to explain the problem and provide a viable solution. It is my practice to never complain about what I'm not willing to change. This is my attempt to do just that.

POLICING
IN FAITH

A Discussion About The Police,
For The Police, and
The People They Serve

Chapter 1: Positively Identifying the Son of God

Whether we like it or not, law enforcement plays a vital role in the Word of God. A prime example is the crucifixion. When you think about the crucifixion, you typically only focus on Jesus, and rightfully so. But when you closely examine those present, you'll soon discover law enforcement played an integral role.

If you were to comparatively investigate the mitigating circumstances surrounding the crucifixion – today - it would be similar to that of a lethal injection execution. Today executions take place inside prison compounds which means both the warden and prison staff are present. Those in attendance, i.e., the prison staff, would be the first to actually witness an inmate's execution. Such was the case at Jesus' execution also commonly referred to as the crucifixion. A prison official was present and witnessed the crucifixion of the Lord Jesus Christ. And though we probably never thought about the crucifixion in that regard, something more significant occurred at the time of the Lord's death that we should also consider. Luke 23:44-47 says,

> "Now it was about the sixth hour, and there was darkness over all the earth until the ninth hour. Then the sun was darkened, and the veil of the temple was torn in two. And when Jesus had cried out with a loud voice, He said, "Father, into Your hands I commit My spirit." Having said this, He breathed His last. So, when the centurion saw what had happened, he glorified God, saying, "Certainly this was a righteous Man!""

As you can see, *a centurion positively identified the Lord as the Son of God* and thus began to glorify God as a result.

This is significant because ordinarily, in Christian circles, most believe that Joseph, the wealthy council member, who offered to pay for the Lord's funeral expenses, was the first person to positively identify the Lord. Some will even argue that Mary Magdalene, or the two disciples, who encountered the Lord on the road to Emmaus, were the first. And though all came in contact with the Lord after His execution/resurrection, neither were the first to actually positively identify that Jesus was the Son of God. And this is where law enforcement comes into play.

Again, Luke 23:44-47 reads,

> "... [when Jesus]...said, "Father, into Your hands I commit My spirit." Having... breathed His last...the centurion [seeing]...what...happened...glorified God, saying, "Certainly this was a righteous Man!"

So, as you can see, the centurion (i.e., law enforcement officer - LEO) was the first person to positively identify the Lord. But to be sure, it should also be noted that the same account of the Lord's death appears in the gospel of Mark. Only in Mark's account, the centurion says, **"Truly this Man was the Son of God."** (Mark 15:39) But why is establishing law enforcement as the first to positively ID the Lord so significant? Because it's not just the fact that they were the first, it's what happened BECAUSE they did.

According to scripture, BECAUSE this prison official positively identified Jesus, he glorified God. But what does that mean?

The Amplified Version describes his response as, **'honoring, thanking and praising [God].'** When you combine the Amplified Version in context with the New King James Version of Luke and Mark's account, the account could now read:

> **'...And Jesus cried out with a loud voice, and breathed His last. Then the veil of the temple was torn in two from top to bottom. ³⁹ So when the centurion, who stood opposite Him, saw that [Jesus] cried out...and breathed His last... [the prison guard] glorified [honored, thanked and praised] God, saying, "Truly this Man was the Son of God!"'** *(Author paraphrase)*

This lets us know that when he realized that Jesus was the Son of God, he immediately thanked and praised God. If this were to happen today, this would be the same as an atheist prison guard being suddenly convinced of God's existence because of an inmate's execution. So much so, that immediately afterward he begins to publicly thank and acknowledge that he now believes in God. That. Is. Powerful.

But let's recap to ensure you get the full picture of who this centurion was. His unit had been assigned to Jesus' crucifixion. When you read of the account, you'll discover that this same unit was also responsible for scourging Jesus.

Scourging was routinely done prior to a crucifixion and often resulted in skin removal. Thus, Jesus would have been stripped naked, tied to a post and mercilessly flogged on His back, buttocks, and legs. This unit was a part of the order the unit had been given.

It should also be noted that this unit were also the ones who would strip, robe, and forcefully embed a crown of thorns into Jesus' head. They also bowed their knees, mocked, and spat on Jesus. It should also be stated that after His death, this very unit also saw **'the veil of the temple...torn in two from top to bottom; [saw].. the earth quake, and [saw] the rocks...split, [52] [They also witnessed] graves...open; and [saw] many bodies of the saints who had fallen asleep [be] raised [from the dead]; [53] and [saw first hand dead bodies come] out of the graves after His resurrection, [and also witnessed those same once dead, risen bodies go] into the holy city...'**

They SAW it. As we just read, the centurion was the first to positively identify as the Son of God. Yet prior to that, his unit were the very ones ordered to carry out lethal force against Jesus.

One would argue they were simply following orders. That is true. However, they were not ordered to put a scarlet robe on Jesus. They were not ordered to put a crown of thorns on His head. Neither were they order to bow their knees or to mock Him. They did that on their own.

Surely the centurion did not order them to cry, **"Hail, King of the Jews!"** Neither were they ordered to spit on Jesus and strike Him on the head. They were just that type of soldier (LEO). This is *how they* carried out orders. They didn't show discretion or restraint. There was no honor in their actions. They were brutal. They were cruel. Although one could argue that they were simply carrying out an order and had nothing to do with the fact that 'the people' decided that Jesus should be crucified, the way they conducted the crucifixion is indicative to who they were as men and as officers of the law. The fact that they taunted and tortured Jesus while carrying out the order speaks volumes. That is the type of men and soldiers they were. Brutal. Cruel. Torturous. Can the same be said of you?

I started drafting this book in 2019. However, this chapter wasn't written until February 2021. In January 2021, less than six days into the new year, more than 35 officers had been positively identified as participants in the insurrection that took place at the U.S. Capitol. Less than 30 days later, the Washington Post reported that 992 people had been shot and killed by police. [1] And by that time, the Black Lives Matter movement had gained traction and had successfully managed to divert several million out of police budgets and redirected those funds into community-based alternatives. Yet here we see the first person whose eternal salvation was forever changed - after the death of Jesus - was in fact, someone in law enforcement. Could God be sending us a message? Or better yet, could this be a clarion call *to* law enforcement?

Though we'll get into this later, the dichotomy is that...

Jesus Himself was a victim of police brutality.
Not only that, but He too was wrongfully convicted and sentenced to death. And what's even more shocking is that the Lord Jesus Christ was posthumously exonerated by none other than law enforcement.

That intel itself is a message that we, the people and those in law enforcement should seriously consider which brings us to our next topic which is this: **What happens to those in law enforcement, when they themselves break the law but later want to confess their wrongdoing?** I pose this question because once that centurion/prison official/guard realized that Jesus was the Son of God, what should he have done? Because remember Jesus had been wrongfully convicted and executed. So, what could or should that officer have done?

CHAPTER TAKE-AWAY: Law enforcement was present at the most crucial, beneficial, pivotable, notable, and life-changing moment in world history, and one officer's eternal salvation came as a result of openly and publicly identifying and thereby posthumously exonerating Jesus Christ as the Son of God.

SOURCES

1-"Fatal Force: Police Shootings Database." *The Washington Post*, WP Company, 22 Jan. 2020.

Chapter 2: Officer Suicides

What happens to those in law enforcement when they themselves break the law but later want to admit to their wrongdoing? The answer to our question is simple. If said officer is a Christian, then he or she must follow the biblical policies and procedures found in scripture. And though that should be painstakingly clear, one can only assume that the right thing to do would also be to notify the appropriate investigative agencies. One could assume that but what if said agencies are corrupt? What if Internal Affairs (IA) are eternally unfaithful in the sense that those under their auspices doubt their trustworthiness? Such was the case with a Louisiana police officer who 'served in Afghanistan and Iraq' [1] who committed suicide 'in protest against police brutality'. [2] In his 16-minute recorded suicide letter, he forthrightly stated officers had no right to mercilessly brutalize minorities without accountability. In fact, it was their lack of accountability, his words not mine, that led him to take his well-lived life.

His story affirms the question - *What if internal affairs are eternally unfaithful in the sense that they cannot be trusted?* This decorated officer thought it best to take his own life...away from his two sons and from the elementary and middle school students he both served, protected, and loved. This upstanding officer said that he'd rather die than report the misdeeds of his fellow officers to internal affairs, and for that matter, to the Justice Department. Let that sink in for a minute. As a public servant, that officer should have been able to safely share his concerns. Yet he is not here with us today. One can only wonder why.

The Statistics

In November 2019, NAACP and Daytime Emmy award-winning broadcast journalist and talk show host, Tamron Hall, did a segment called, the *'Mental Health Crisis with Police Suicides.'* By that time there had been ten officer suicides in the state of New York that year alone. While thinking about that statistic, I asked myself the obvious question - why? Why would men and women, who according to Title 38 of the United States Code section 902 who'd had been given the right to

> '...enforce Federal laws and rules prescribed under section 901 (such as protecting persons and property); who could enforce

traffic and motor vehicle laws, carry...department-issued weapons and firearms as well as conduct investigations on a state and federal level' [3] - 38 U.S. Code § 902

Why would people, with that level of authority and power, want to take their own lives?

According to Blue H.E.L.P.'s website, a 501(c)3 whose mission is to support families impacted by officer suicides, 173 officers [4] took their lives in 2022. To put that into perspective, that same year, there were '708,001 full-time law enforcement officers employed in the United States.' [5] That means .032% committed suicide, and though a small percentage, one thing we must consider is that one officer has the potential to interact, protect and/or impact hundreds, and quite possibly thousands of civilians throughout his or her tenure which means the likelihood of participating and/or witnessing officer misconduct is highly probable. But what led those 173 to take their own?

Because I was given the assignment to pray for law enforcement and out of that prayer write this book, one could only assume I have the answer. Though I may not have a definitive answer, one thing God impressed upon my heart is that some came to the point of repentance. Some of those who swore to protect and serve their respective communities came to the point where he or she wanted to come clean. Each may have wanted to come clean about crimes they themselves, and/or their fellow officers had committed, while in the line of duty. But again, how could they do so safely when many of the appropriate investigative agencies were incapable of guaranteeing their safety. Not to mention the safety of their loved ones.

So, what happens when a corrupt officer wants to do the right thing? And while we're on the subject...**What happens when a Christian officer wants to do the same?**

Officer Suicides in the Bible

If we were to put ourselves in the shoes of that late officer, the first thing we'd have to do, as a Christian officer, is repent and address the fear of prosecution from higher ranking officers while facing the backlash from our fellow colleagues. Both of which we'll delve into later. But because this officer was contemplating suicide, it's probably best that we first locate instances - in the Bible - of officer suicides. Do such instances exist? Absolutely. Acts 16:25-28 says,

> '...at midnight Paul and Silas were praying and singing hymns to God, and the prisoners were listening...[when] suddenly there was a great earthquake, so that the foundations of the prison were shaken; and immediately all the doors were opened and everyone's chains were loosed. [27] And the keeper of the prison, awaking from sleep and seeing the prison doors open, supposing the prisoners had fled, drew his sword and was about to kill himself. [28] But Paul called with a loud voice, saying, "Do yourself no harm, for we are all here." – New King James Version

In this account, the prison guard was about to commit suicide, but Paul, another wrongfully accused civilian, talked him out of it. Further proving some inmates can have a profound effect on law enforcement. But our assignment is not to prove that profound effect, not yet anyway.

Our assignment is to try to understand why some officers would rather take their own lives. Our assignment for this chapter is to try to see if there's some type of internal ideology behind their actions. With that in mind, let's take a closer look at this officer/guard. Why was his first inclination to kill himself?

According to '...Roman law, a guard who allowed the escape of a prisoner was...to be put to death' on the basis of dereliction of duty. [6] According to Cornell Law School's online Legal Information Institute, dereliction of duty is defined as, '...a person's purposeful or accidental failure to perform an obligation without a valid excuse, especially an obligation attached to his or her job.' [7] Thus, explaining why the guard guarding Paul opted to try to kill himself while on duty. But again, what was the Roman ideology behind his decision, or was this simply the culture of policing?

Roman law states that anyone found guilty of willfully neglecting his or her duty should be put to death in the presence of and/or at the hands of their fellow officers. Therefore, the mindset of this officer, as may be the case with officers today, is that some would rather take their own lives rather than face the ostracism, the banishment, and the lack of support and/or back up from their colleagues. Thankfully, Paul convinced this guard not to harm himself since no dereliction of duty occurred. However, such wasn't the case in 1 Samuel 31 where we find another example of an officer suicide. Here we find the Philistines defeating Israel.

In this instance, we find a Philistine army in hot pursuit of an Israeli king by the name of Saul.

> **'The battle became fierce against Saul [and] the archers hit him, and he was severely wounded...[Saul]...then...said to his armorbearer, "Draw your sword, and thrust me through with it, lest these uncircumcised men come and thrust me through and abuse me." But his armorbearer would not, for he was greatly afraid. Therefore Saul took a sword and fell on it. ⁵And when his armorbearer saw that Saul was dead, he also fell on his sword, and died with him.'**

Swords were the service weapons of the day. Therefore, falling on the sword would be the same as using a service weapon to commit suicide. And thus, we have one instance of a king, who would be analogous to our president today, taking his own life. And though presidents don't enforce laws, he would still be considered a member of law enforcement because apart of his presidential duty is to ensure laws are faithfully executed. [8] Therefore, Saul, the highest-ranking person in his nation, chose to kill himself rather than become a political prisoner of war.

On top of that, we have an armourbearer, who, today, would be akin to the president's chief of staff; yet another member of law enforcement, taking his own life. And thus, in our brief quest to understand the ideology behind Roman/Israeli officer suicides in the Bible, we've discovered that one officer would have rather taken his own life than to be punished and/or ostracized by his fellow officers (Acts 16:25-28) while the other chose to inflict death upon himself rather than to fall into enemy hands (1 Sam. 31:2-5).

Are there other reasons? Absolutely. I'm pretty sure there are those who would rather take their own lives than to betray their badge and the badge of their colleagues and I'm also sure there are those who may not have the wherewithal to hold themselves, let alone their peers, accountable for their criminal behavior. And please don't misunderstand me. I am not condemning or belittling the lives of the officers who are no longer with us. My objective is simple: To provide biblical encouragement and to get to the root of that ideology so that those who are now faced with the same set of circumstances don't take their own God-given lives. So, if you, or someone you know, is having suicidal thoughts...

Pray this with me: Heavenly Father, I don't see a way out. I am ashamed and afraid. I cannot go to prison, and I don't see how I can do the right thing. But if You show me how to navigate through this Heavenly Father, I will do whatever needs to be done. I just ask You for the strength, the courage, and the protection needed, for me and my loved ones to get through this. And Lord, I assure You, I will do the right thing. In Jesus' name.

*The numbers on Blue H.E.L.P. fluctuate regularly and may decrease or increase over time.
** I am not affiliated with, endorsed by or sponsored by BLUE H.E.L.P.

SOURCES

1, 2 - Boyette, Chris. "A Black Sheriff's Deputy in Louisiana Condemned Police Brutality and Institutionalized Racism. Then He Died by Suicide." *CNN*, Cable News Network, 6 Feb. 2021.

3 - "38 U.S. Code § 902 - Enforcement and Arrest Authority of Department Police Officers." *Legal Information Institute*, Legal Information Institute.

4 - "The Numbers." *Blue H.E.L.P.*, 19 Apr. 2021.

5 - Published by Korhonen, Veera. "U.S. Law Enforcement Officers 2022." *Statista*, 5 July 2024.

6 – "BibleGateway." *Acts 16 KJV - - Bible Gateway*.

7 - "Dereliction." *Legal Information Institute*, Legal Information Institute.

8 - "Annotation 16 - Article II." *FindLaw*,

Chapter 3: Civilian Complaint Process

In the previous chapter we discussed the possible ideology behind officer suicides for the sole purpose of trying to prevent future deaths. Our mission going forward is to provide a way out for those LEO's who want to come clean but perhaps may not know how to safely navigate the often dangerous and deadly terrain of the police complaint process. But why is that terrain so dangerous? Let's first take a closer look at the civilian complaint process to see if we can find that answer. Because I reside in the Lone Star State, we'll use Dallas as our template.

Municipal Complaints

Currently, if a resident has a complaint against a Dallas Police Officer there are several ways to file a grievance. You can:

1. Go to the police station and speak with the Supervisor.
2. File an External Administrative Complaint Form online, or...
3. Report your issue to Internal Affairs. [1]

What's striking is that the Dallas Police Department's website goes to painstaking lengths to point out that 'a detective will come get you and help walk you through the entire process.' Though intended to be helpful to some, especially for those filing *officer misconduct* complaints, this verbiage can be interpreted as intimidating. The site also states that a 'supervisor will help...initiate the complaint process and provide...a complaint form to complete.' [2] Again, to some, especially for those filing *officer misconduct* complaints, this again may come across as useless; especially, since most Supervisors – on any job and in any industry – are instructed to build rapport and have a good working, professional relationship with their counterparts and/or direct reports. Therefore, to file a complaint with such a person can appear to be an exercise in futility.

Inasmuch, if after submitting a grievance, should the civilian complainant be displeased with the results of the complaint that just so happened to be internally reviewed by said officer's colleagues, they are then instructed to contact the City of Dallas' Office of Community Oversight. However, it should be noted that according to the National Association for Civilian Oversight of Law Enforcement's (NACOLE) Executive Summary, that of the 166 civilian oversight agencies operating in 140 jurisdictions nationwide, less than half – 44.5 percent - have authority to recommend discipline on misconduct cases. [3]

Their report also mentions that legislators are giving more credence to civilian review boards. The legislation mentioned in their 2016 report came in the form of Title I Subtitle A Section 104 (22) of the pending George Floyd Policing Act (H.R. 1280) which calls for, '...creating civilian review boards.' [4] This act would allow civilians to escalate their complaint while at the same time making way for the violating officer's name to be listed in a nationwide database for misconduct.

State Complaints

Should a civilian opt to bypass the Office of Community Oversight and instead attempt to personally escalate their complaint by contacting state officials, according to the State of Texas Attorney General's website, they...

> 'should...report [their grievance] ...to the Internal Affairs section of the department or to the police chief. If [the person isn't] satisfied with the response... [they receive there, then they are then instructed to] ... contact the mayor, city manager and/or city council members.' [5]

Therefore, to date, in the state of Texas, if a *civilian* has an officer complaint, the state Attorney General's office will not be able to assist.

Federal Complaints

If, however, the citizen's complaint is vetted by municipal and state authorities, it could go to the federal level but only if it has met the following criteria:

1) The officer would have had to violate the complainant's federal (civil) rights, and...

2) The violating officer's agency had to have received federal funding.

Why is this important? Though we'll dive deeper in later chapters, unless the officer(s) and/or agency violates the protocols, as prescribed in the 'anti-discrimination provision of the Omnibus Crime Control and Safe Streets Act of 1968, and Title VI of the Civil Rights Acts of 1964, which forbids discrimination on the basis of race, color, sex or national origin by agencies receiving federal funds' [6], there's no civil punitive action that can be done, and in most cases, neither can anything be done criminally.

Therefore, in answering our question: **Why is the terrain so dangerous for those wishing to report their fellow officers' criminal misconduct?** As you can see the complaint process for a civilian on a municipal level is often intimidating and indiscreet and usually leads to nothing meaningful. And if the complainant is dissatisfied with the results, they are then rerouted to another agency which on the surface can appear to prove the illegitimacy of the complaint. All the while said civilian runs the risk of police retaliation.

On a state level, there is nothing, in the State of Texas, that the Attorney General can do. And on a federal level, the complaint would have to go through the proper channels (i.e., municipal and/or state) in order to make it to the state's U.S. Attorney which means the likelihood of police misconduct complaints reaching punitive and/or prosecutory levels, historically, has been highly unlikely. Which again, leaves said civilian running the risk of being subject to intimidation and/or retaliation in which case, said civilian would also have to return to the same department in which the complaint was lodged to seek protection. Further explaining why, the complaint process terrain is so dangerous.

SOURCES

1,2 - "File A Complaint." *Dallas Police Department*.

3, 4 - "Conduct of Law Enforcement Agencies." *The United States Department of Justice*, 21 Apr. 2021.

5- "What The Attorney General Can Do For You." *Liberty and Justice for Texas | Office of the Attorney General*.

6 - Wikipedia contributors. "Civil Rights Act of 1964." *Wikipedia, The Free Encyclopedia*. Wikipedia, The Free Encyclopedia, 13 Mar. 2022. Web. 19 Mar. 2022.

Chapter 4: The Code of Silence

Now that you understand the civilian complaint process, you can better understand why the officer complaint process is so dangerous. But again, why is it so dangerous for one officer to report the misconduct of a fellow officer? In order to answer that question, we'll first look into the reporting process.

Internal Affairs

Without going into great detail, Internal Affairs (IA) is where officer misconduct is reported. The job of Internal Affairs is 'to investigate incidents and possible suspicions of law-breaking and professional misconduct.' [1] Coincidentally, the same department that handles civilian complaints is also the same department that investigates interoffice employee complaints as well. Thus, helping you better understand why the complaint process is so dangerous.

Officers who chose to report misconduct are investigated by other high-ranking officers. Therefore, in previous chapters, when the question was posed: **What if Internal Affairs is eternally unfaithful in the sense that those under their auspices doubt their trustworthiness?** It's because complaints are handled internally. Consequently, complaining officers run the risk of reporting the misdeeds of their fellow comrades to those who are familiar with the accused. Familiar in the sense that they may be directly and/or indirectly connected – professionally and/or personally - to the officer(s) listed in the complaint. And though this office is required by law to remain unbiased, the probability of the complaint not getting back to the accused or other officers *familiar* with the accused, is highly improbable. Further explaining why the process is so dangerous. But why do I continue to use the word dangerous?

Because when you think about it, every company has a department where employees can report fraud, waste, abuse, and misconduct. You can always contact your Human Resources department to complain about a fellow co-worker or Supervisor who violates company policy. At best, the worst complaints involve discrimination or harassment. But what if one officer witnessed a fellow officer plant evidence that cost someone their freedom? What if an officer willfully shot a suspect without cause, or worse, what if an officer witnessed a murder? The nature of their complaint can pay a heavy toll on the lives of the complaining officer and the accused because the accused runs the risk of losing not only their job but quite possibly their freedom. Again, further explaining why the complaint process is so dangerous and why most opt to abide by what's often referred to as the code of silence.

Keeping the Code of Silence vs. Violating Your Spiritual and Contractual Obligations

The code of silence is defined as 'the practice of not disclosing important or vital information by members of a group, as due to the threat of violence, reprisal, being branded as a traitor, or an inherent sense of honor.' [2] More times than not, those in law enforcement either choose or fail to disclose vital details about the criminal behavior and/or activities of their fellow officers. This not only applies to verbal silence but can also be demonstrated by filing a false report, falsifying evidence, allowing spoliation of evidence, and/or committing perjury, to name a few. And though disturbing, according to a Rutgers Journal of Law & Public Policy article entitled, *'Whistleblowing and the Police'* by Roberta Ann Johnson where a retired Minneapolis Police Department Chief, stated that those who do report misconduct are often labeled as a snitch and '...are scorned, shunned, excluded, condemned, harassed, and almost invariably, cast out." [3] "The Washington Post also reported [that whistleblowers also], end up on a 'hit list' that can result in unwanted transfers, pay docking, unfavorable assignments, personnel complaints, demotions, terminations...and other retaliatory measures." [4]

You can better understand why the police complaint process is so dangerous. Because when you think about it, to be scorned, shunned, harassed, transferred, docked, demoted, possibly terminated, or worse, places officers in precarious and unsafe situations, which is why most remain silent. It almost seems as if there's safety in silence. But if you're a Christian law enforcement agent, silence is never an option because as a child of God you're obligated to tell the truth - both *to God* and *to man*.

You're obligated to God because as a child of God, you agreed:

1. **To serve the Truth.** If Jesus is your Lord and Savior, then you agreed to serve and live for Him. Jesus is not only the Christ but He's also "...the way, the truth, and the life." (John 14:6) That said, you also agreed...

2. **To be led by the Spirit of truth.** If you are filled with the Holy Spirit, then the Spirit of truth "...will guide you into all truth..." (John 16:13) which means He may also lead you to disclose damaging information about your colleagues. But even more importantly, as a child of God you also agreed...

3. **To live by the word of truth.** Because you are filled with the Spirit of truth, then as a follower of Jesus - who is the Truth - then your job as a law enforcement agent is to enforce the law *truthfully*. 'God has sanctified you by His truth [because His] word is truth." (John 17:17) However, if in the past you kept the code, then perhaps there's not enough of God's word (i.e., the truth) in you.

It should also be noted that you are also obligated to honor your word *to man*.

When you joined the force, you signed a personnel contract in which you agreed to adhere to departmental policy which includes your adherence to notify your Supervisor or Internal Affairs, the Office of Professional Standards, or depending upon your city/state, the appropriate reporting agency, of any internal misconduct. To NOT do so is a blatant violation of your contract and could for all intents and purposes nullify not only your personnel agreement, but also the oath you took which could invariably jeopardize your right to serve. Therefore, the question now becomes: Are you breaking municipal, state, and/or federal law by keeping the code? The short answer is yes. Simply because you failed to abide by the terms stipulated in your contract, which include you agreeing to report misconduct.

But before you get upset with me, please know that I did not draft your contract, nor did I write the policies. Your department did. And your signature represents your agreement to both uphold and adhere to the terms and policies written therein. But should you choose to allow the *unwritten code of silence* to override departmental policy, your contractual obligation, and/or state and federal law, that's totally between you, your superiors, and more importantly, your God.

With that being said, you now have a decision to make: Are you going to truthfully enforce the written laws of the land or abide by the unwritten, illegal code of silence?

To help you make that decision…

Pray this with me: Heavenly Father, though I've kept the code of silence in the past, I did not realize I was also violating departmental policy and the written contract I agreed to. If nothing else Heavenly Father, I want to honor my contractual agreement, my word to You, and live a truthful, integrous life. So, I ask You to help me speak up when necessary and report what's needed. In Jesus' name.

Kudos to you for praying that prayer. If you're serious about your decision, then you have to consider the following: ***What happens now that you want to break the code and do the right thing?***

Doing the Right Thing

In the book of Mark, chapter 15, we find the answer to our question. Verses 33-39 says:

> '…**when the sixth hour had come, there was darkness over the whole land until the ninth hour.** [34] **And at the ninth hour Jesus cried out with a loud voice, saying,** "Eloi, Eloi, lama sabachthani?" **which is translated,** "My God, My God, why have You forsaken Me?" …[37] **And Jesus cried out with a loud voice, and breathed His last.** [38] **Then the veil of the temple was torn in two from top to bottom.** [39] **So when the centurion, who stood opposite Him, saw that He cried out like this and breathed His last…he glorified [honored, thanked and praised] God, saying, "Truly this Man was the Son of God!"** – Mark 15:33-39 NKJV

Let me preface this by saying that the centurion mentioned here was from Rome. Rome was polytheistic which means it's likely that he believed in more than one god. Therefore, it's safe to assume that this centurion did not believe that Jesus was the Son of God *prior* to His crucifixion. Yet that didn't stop him from publicly acknowledging Jesus' true identity. This is an important piece in answering our question about what happens when you want to break the code.

After Jesus' wrongful execution, the Amplified version of this account says that '...**the centurion...said, "Indeed, without question, [Jesus] was upright (just and innocent)!"** Notice, the Bible doesn't say that the centurion, who today would be classified as a lieutenant, was off duty when he made that statement. Neither does it say after a time of personal reflection or after seeking legal counsel. The Bible clearly states that after, **'having seen what had taken place [which would have been at the time of the crucifixion] ...the centurion said...[Jesus]...was innocent!"** Right there, on the spot, in front of, **'the throngs that had gathered to'** witness Jesus' execution, this centurion/prison guard/lieutenant/law enforcement official publicly acknowledged the Lord's innocence. But why is that so important and what does it have to do with doing the right thing and the code of silence?

Criminal Charges Against the Lord

To give you a bit of a backstory, you must first understand the nature of Jesus' case. The Sanhedrin, which consisted of two classes of Jewish courts, [5] indicted Jesus on several charges. Namely, destruction of property, tax evasion, blasphemy, and criminal impersonation. We know these were the charges because Matthew 26:59-66 lays out three of the four when it reads,

> '...**the chief priests, the elders, and all the council sought false testimony against Jesus to put Him to death, but found none. Even though many false witnesses came forward, they found none. But at last two false witnesses came forward and said, "This Fellow said, "I am able to destroy the temple of God and to build it in three days."** – Matthew 26:59-61 NKJV

In other words, these two witnesses falsely accused Jesus of threatening to destroy a historic landmark. And even if their testimony were proven true, the charge did not warrant death. Not to mention, no report of an attempt was ever reported, which meant those charges should have been dismissed due to lack of evidence. But again, it was not.

Jesus was also charged with tax evasion. This charge was solely based upon a public discussion the Lord had with both the religious and legal authorities in Matthew 22:15-21 which says,

> **'Then the Pharisees went and plotted how they might entangle [Jesus] in His talk… [and they asked Him]…"Teacher, we know that You are true, and teach the way of God in truth; nor do You…regard the person of men. Tell us…is it lawful to pay taxes to Caesar, or not?"** [18] **But Jesus perceived their wickedness, and said,** "Why do you test Me, you hypocrites? [19] Show Me the tax money." **So, they brought Him a denarius.** [20] **And He said to them,** "Whose image and inscription is this?" [21] **They said to Him, "Caesar's" And He said to them,** "Render therefore to Caesar the things that are Caesar's, and to God the things that are God's."

Clearly, the Lord didn't instruct the crowd not to pay their taxes and neither did He fail to pay His own because in Matthew 17:24-27,

> **'…when…those who received the temple tax came to Peter [a member of Jesus' staff asked Peter] …"Does your [Boss] not pay the temple tax?"…[Peter responded]…"Yes." And when he had come into the house, Jesus anticipated him, saying,** "What do you think, Simon [Peter]? From whom do the kings of the earth take customs [or taxes], from their sons or from strangers?" [26] **Peter said to Him, "From strangers." Jesus said to him,** "Then the sons are free. [27] Nevertheless, lest we offend them, go to the sea, cast in a hook, and take the fish that comes up first. And when you have opened its mouth, you will find a piece of money; take that and give it to them for Me and you." *(author paraphrase)*

As you can see, the Lord *never instructed anyone not to pay their taxes* and even went to painstaking lengths to pay not only His taxes, but those of His staff. But that was irrelevant to His accusers. And thus, further proves two of the four charges were false. But it doesn't stop there.

When it came to the other two charges, blasphemy, and criminal impersonation, we find the same pattern in Matthew 26:62-66 which says,

> '...the high priest...said to [Jesus], "Do You answer nothing? What is it these men testify against You?" [63] But Jesus kept silent. And the high priest answered and said "...Tell us if You are the Christ, the Son of God!" Jesus said to him, "It is as you said...Then the high priest [said]... "He has spoken blasphemy! What further need do we have of witnesses?"

Though the Lord acknowledged His true identity, His confession did not warrant a sentence worthy of the death penalty; only because even today, blasphemy is considered a misdemeanor. Therefore, in an effort to justify their wrongdoing, they charged Jesus with two felonies; tax evasion and criminal impersonation which today is only a first-degree class C felony. And it is this charge that marries the centurion's actions with what officers can do today.

Criminal impersonation occurs when a person,

> '(a) Assumes a false identity and does an act in his or her assumed character with intent to defraud another or for any other unlawful purpose; or
>
> (b) Pretends to be a representative of some person, organization or a public servant and does an act in his/her pretended capacity with intent to defraud another or for any other unlawful purpose.'
> [6]

In Jesus' case, that person and/or organization would have been God and His kingdom. Thus, when asked if He (Jesus) was the Son of God, the Lord incriminated Himself by admitting His true identity which ultimately led Him to be criminally prosecuted and sentenced to death. But remember, He was sentenced to death because *the authorities* accused Him of criminal impersonation. *They* said that He wasn't the Son of God. In fact, this was the basis of *their* blasphemy and criminal impersonation cases. Yet when we find the centurion (lieutenant) positively identifying Jesus as the Son of God and readily admitting "without question" to Jesus' innocence. So, now you can better understand why those charges were false, and thus answers our question - *What happens when an officer wants to break the code of silence and do the right thing? He or she should immediately, openly, and publicly acknowledge what they know.*

Though this officer had no need to report the misconduct of a fellow officer, his public acknowledgment of Christ's identity let other officers, officials, and those responsible for the Lord's death know that the Lord was innocent. Which today, by default, would have led to an internal investigation of the aforementioned parties and thus would have resulted in a posthumous exoneration for the Lord.

Officers who want to report misconduct should follow the centurion's example by immediately and publicly acknowledging what they know. Unfortunately, most fail to do so in a timely fashion thus resulting in wrongful convictions, or worse, death. An example of this can be found with Officer Woods and Malcolm X.

The Harmful Results of Keeping the Code

In February 2021 the North Star, an independent, grassroots blog, reported that "retired NYPD officer Raymond Wood detailed the role he played with the New York Police Department and the FBI in the murder of Malcolm X", [7] a popular Muslim minister and human rights activist. "The Washington Post reported that in a...

> '2011 letter by...now-dead officer, Raymond A. Wood...Wood had been compelled by his supervisors at the New York Police Department to coax two members of Malcolm X's security team into committing crimes, leading to their arrests just a few days before the assassination. They were then unable to secure the entry to New York's Audubon Ballroom, where Malcolm X had been speaking when he was killed... [Woods wrote]...the letter shortly after being diagnosed with stomach cancer [but] stipulated to his cousin that he did not want his involvement to be made public until after his death. His cancer went into remission in 2012, and he did not die until Nov. 24, 2020.' [8]

As you can see, this officer kept the code of silence and carried the knowledge that not only had he been used to divert Malcolm X's security detail, but he also knowingly allowed three men to remain in prison, one of whom died while the other two served more than 20 years for crimes they didn't commit*. It wasn't until after those two gentlemen had been paroled that Officer Woods wrote his confession which then would not be read until a decade later.

Malcolm X was assassinated February 21, 1965, which means Officer Woods carried that secret for 46 years and it didn't go public until 10 years after his death.

The centurion went public moments after Jesus' death while this officer waited 46 years after Malcolm Xs to report the misconduct of his Supervisor and the FBI.

46 years is the equivalent to 16,790 days for the three men wrongfully convicted of the crime. And this is only <u>one</u> instance of <u>one officer</u> failing to report the wrongdoing of a fellow officer.

Let's for a moment think about the 173 officers mentioned earlier, who took their own lives. What if they too had similar knowledge? What if each were privy to a fellow officer planting evidence, using excessive force, or murdering innocent civilians thus resulting in hundreds of years of imprisonment and/or deaths? Did forever holding their peace and not immediately sharing what they knew, ultimately drive them to resting in it (peace)?

And what about the other 697,195 full-time law enforcement personnel currently employed in the US today? How many countless secrets have been kept by those who swore to protect and to serve? And not only swore to protect and serve their respective communities but also vowed to truthfully serve their Lord and Savior Jesus Christ?

The irony of it all, is that had Christian officers, such as Mr. Wood, been on duty during Jesus' crucifixion, it is highly probable that they too would have said nothing. Instead of immediately and publicly acknowledging Jesus' innocence, they too would have likely withheld that little bit of unclassified information until after their passing. All the while, continuing to protect and to serve while confessing Jesus as their Lord and Savior.

The fact that the centurion, an unbelieving law enforcement agent, publicly acknowledged that Jesus was wrongfully executed is something that all badge-wearing Christian officers should know. Maybe now they will. But let's not think it happenstance that God put that information in the Bible for the purpose of just providing historical data. The Bible is the living Word of the living God. And if you're in law enforcement, then His Word should serve as a living template and should be used as a living professional and moral guidepost for your life.

If you have knowledge of misconduct, then as a disciple of Jesus Christ, it is your duty to tell the truth and to *openly* and *publicly acknowledge what you know.* You pledged your allegiance to God therefore your first allegiance is to Him and to His Son, Jesus Christ. Your second allegiance is to your spouse, your children and your loved ones run a close third. The brotherhood falls thereafter. If your first allegiance goes against what God has said in His Word, then you have another decision to make. Will you honor your allegiance to God and His Son, or will you put your fellow officers first? To help you make that decision...

Pray this with me: Heavenly Father, I know You are my God and Jesus is my Savior and Lord. As Your son/daughter, I know my first allegiance is to You but Lord, I know information about my fellow officers, that if I disclose, could jeopardize my life and the lives of those I love. But if I don't report what I know, my silence will continue to devastate the lives of others, who quite possibly are my brothers and sisters in Christ. So, Heavenly Father, I ask You to give me the protection, the courage, and the direction I need to do what I know is right in Your sight. I ask this in Jesus' name. Amen.

Before we move on to the next chapter, it bears mentioning that Malcolm X died in 1965 which means 47 years had passed before Mr. Wood's cancer went into remission in 2012. What if God healed Officer Wood so that he could walk out what we're discussing today? What if God wanted Mr. Wood to be an example of His healing and redemptive power? We can assume this was the case because year after year God gave him time, space, and opportunity to confess his involvement which would have been considered as an act to make it right. Unfortunately, he refused and died at the age of 87 carrying that secret to his grave.

But again, this only demonstrates the *goodness of God* because God gave him 8 years after his remission to make it right. Yet he did nothing. And that's just one officer. There are so many, like Mr. Muhammad Aziz, Mujahid Abdul Halim, and Khalil Islam, who are serving time for someone else's crime, namely those in law enforcement. And though that concept is not foreign to God, because *His Son served ours*, it goes without saying that keeping the code of silence has devastating, long-term effects.

As a domestic violence and violent crime survivor, I understand the code of silence all too well. As a woman of God, I also understand how that silence weighs on the spirit. And though, as an officer, your physical safety is important, that silence also pays a heavy price on your soul. And it is for this reason that we now must shift away from the reporting side of the code of silence into the spiritual effects of it. Because if you continue to remain silent, not only are you violating departmental policy on top of failing to adhere to the terms stipulated in your contract, but you're also in direct opposition with the Lord Jesus Christ Himself. Only because such silence is interpreted as a failure to confess your sins which would also mean you are failing to repent which would thereby mean you are not acknowledging Jesus as Your Lord. He's merely your Savior. This is why it was so important for you to pray that prayer. It was important to get your heart into a place where you're able to receive the *direction* you'll need to safely move forward, professionally, privately, and more importantly, spiritually. However, before we do, I need to preface this by saying the remainder of this book will be hard-hitting. Meaning, it will provide the necessary and mandatory *correction* you need to face what lie ahead...professionally, privately, and spiritually.

*Muhammad A. Aziz and Khalil Islam were both exonerated on November 16, 2021.

SOURCES

1 - Wikipedia contributors. "Internal affairs (law enforcement)." *Wikipedia, The Free Encyclopedia*. Wikipedia, The Free Encyclopedia, 1 Jul. 2021. Web. 21 Aug. 2021.

2 - "Code of Silence." *The Free Dictionary*, Farlex.

3, 4 - "Whistleblowing and the Police - Rutgers Journal of Law & Public Policy." *Rutgers Policy Journal*.

5 - Wikipedia contributors. "Sanhedrin." *Wikipedia, The Free Encyclopedia*. Wikipedia, The Free Encyclopedia, 24 May. 2022. Web. 11 Jun. 2022.

6 - *RCW 9A.60.040: Criminal Impersonation in the First Degree.*

7 - King, Shaun. "NYPD Officer Admits He Played a Role in the Murder of Malcolm X." *NYPD Officer Admits He Played a Role in the Murder of Malcolm X*, The North Star with Shaun King, 22 Feb. 2021.

8 - Trent, Sydney. "Malcolm X's Family Reveals Letter They Say Shows NYPD, FBI Assassination Involvement." *The Washington Post*, WP Company, 22 Feb. 2021.

Chapter 5: Correction Byway of Repentance

Again, it was important to get your heart into a place where you're able to receive the *direction* you'll need to safely move forward spiritually, personally and with your career in law enforcement. Therefore, the next order of business is to provide the *correction* you'll also need in order to get there. So, let's dive right in.

Correction in Hebrew is defined as 'discipline of the moral nature.' It's also described as 'chastening', of which you're about to receive. And though God is using me to correct you, it is important that you know that this was *not* my idea. Though I once held law enforcement in high disdain, I also hold a high level of respect for the profession. Therefore, when I was given the assignment of correcting career professionals, such as yourself, I did not take it lightly which is why I thought it was important to reiterate that this is *not* something I wanted to do. But it is my God-given assignment, nonetheless, and as such, there are two things you should know going forward.

1. God is not only your God, but He is also your Father, and...
2. You are God's child, even if you are an adult one.

With that in mind, let's take a look at Hebrews 12:5-11 which says,

> "⁵ **My son, do not despise the chastening of the LORD, nor be discouraged when you are rebuked by Him; ⁶ For whom the LORD loves He chastens, and scourges every son whom He receives." ⁷ If you endure chastening, God deals with you as with sons; for what son is there whom a father does not chasten? ⁸ But if you are without chastening, of which all have become partakers, then you are illegitimate and not sons.**
>
> **⁹ Furthermore, we have had human fathers who corrected us, and we paid them respect. Shall we not much more readily be in subjection to the Father of spirits and live? ¹⁰ For they indeed for a few days chastened us as seemed best to them, but He for our profit, that we may be partakers of His holiness. ¹¹ Now no chastening seems to be joyful for the present, but painful; nevertheless, afterward it yields the**

peaceable fruit of righteousness to those who have been trained by it.'

As you can see the LORD chastens those whom He loves and those whom He considers sons. If you've ever wondered if God loves you, let me say without question, your Heavenly Father does. The mere fact that He led you to read this book proves it. And because He loves you so much, He wants to ensure that you receive the chastening and the correction you need in order to grow spiritually and develop professionally. So go into this understanding that both *chastening, and correction are for your good.* No, it won't be *joyful* and yes, it will be *painful*. But by the end of the book, you can rest assured that you'll be a better person, spouse, parent, law enforcement agent, and more importantly, child of God.

As a law enforcement professional, I think you can understand and appreciate corrective action. Seeing as how the bulk of your responsibilities include either *directly correcting* the action(s), and/or behavior(s) of others, contribute to corrective actions in some administrative capacity or the fact that you provide *indirect correction* which involves you taking civilians into custody to possibly receive criminal *corrective actions* which may include being sentenced to *correctional facilities*.

I mention this now because, ironically, you're about to undergo a *spiritual correction* of sorts which means you now have the right to remain silent and know that going forward, anything you say, can, and will be used against you…in the eyes of God. With that being said, our question for this chapter will be: **What is it about you that needs to be corrected?**

Well, in answering that question, unless you've arrived at Christlike perfection, there could be any number of things. My only assignment is to correct your insistent allegiance to the code of silence. I've also been tasked to lead you into repentance. In order to get you there, we must first look at the culture of policing.

Again, at the time of this writing, the Department of Justice have launched several civil rights abuse investigations against police departments nationwide in the year 2021 alone. Abuses which include illegal strip and body cavity searches, use of force, police brutality, robbery, and drug planting, to name a few. Because these offenses occurred within racially marginalized communities, one has to ask the question: ***What if these investigations, along with the Black Lives Matter and the Defund the Police movements, are the direct result and a combination of both silent complicity and a lack of repentance?*** In other words, what if your insistent allegiance to *not* report wrongdoing brought about this turn of events? Simply because you, and your peers, failed to repent and do something about the rotten apples within your ranks. Or maybe you think you don't have to? Maybe because of the nature of your profession, you believe you're exempt from repentance, which would thereby justify your silence. One could make that argument but then one would be wrong. So, for the sake of argument let's address that question: ***Are law enforcement personnel required to repent or does the profession exempt you from it?***

To Repent or Not to Repent?

As someone in law enforcement, you'll probably agree that as a whole, the profession isn't known for being empathetic or repentant. In fact, as a career professional, you probably pride yourself on your mental toughness and your ability to disengage emotionally. You believe that since you didn't commit the crime, you have nothing to repent and/or apologize for. And if by chance you did commit a crime and do feel some sort of remorse, you mistakenly believe that because you were legally justified, you're exempt from repentance and thereby only feel sorry for your actions which is fine professionally but spiritually, you're in danger. That's because as a Christian law enforcement agent, you're required to repent. And just know, there's a difference between apologizing, feeling sorry, and repentance.

Sorry or sorrow means 'to be distressed, to be sad or to be in heaviness.' [1] Say for instance, you did something in which you were found to be legally justified. Later you begin to feel sorry for what you did. The object of the sorrow would be you which means your sorrow comes from a selfish place because you're only concerned about how you feel. It has nothing to do with the parties involved.

On the other hand, an apology, which is defined as 'a formal justification, defense, excuse, an admission of error or discourtesy accompanied by an expression of regret,' [2] tends to focus on *you* explaining why *you* did what *you* did. Thus, an apology allows *you* to feel sorry while trying to justify or provide an explanation for *your* actions. Therefore, if you did apologize byway of partially reporting an incident or by defending and excusing the actions of your peers out of sorrow or regret, then no, you did not repent. Simply because there was no change in your thoughts and behavior. And thus, as God's child, you have to do better. The better comes in the form of repentance.

The Point of Repentance

Earlier we touched on the increase of officer suicides and asked ourselves, why? Though we'll probably never know, one can only speculate that before they took their lives, each quite possibly came to the point of repentance. If you've never come to the point of repentance or don't understand what that means, allow me to explain my own.

It was the morning after my shooting, after having convinced my son to attend keep his probation appointment, I began to cry and pray profusely when before I knew it, out of my spirit I asked God to forgive me. I asked Him to because I realized that not only did my son have to watch as a lie in a pool of blood after my house was shot up with multiple military grade AR shells, but God had to watch while someone tried to take my life. I asked Him to forgive the fact that *I had put myself* in that situation. Though I still to this day do not know why I was shot, I took sole responsibility because a few weeks prior, while in a time of prayer, I felt the presence of evil. It was as if I knew something awfully bad was about to happen. At which point, God let me know that I needed to move, and I needed to do it quickly. No, I didn't hear an audible voice but knew inside, He was speaking to me.

At the time, my son and I were living in a rat, termite, and wasp infected duplex, located next door to a dope house. I'd been unemployable for several years and was living off college grants, child support and food stamps; all of which totaled less than $475 a month. So, when I heard the Lord tell me that I needed to move, I felt as if I couldn't, because my only option was to move in with friends and family, of whom I'd already worn out my welcome. God then placed my mother on my heart. I immediately rejected that thought because my mother and I hardly ever spoke so when I heard, *"Ask your mother if you can live with her.,"* I didn't think it was possible because she'd rejected me several times before. I then began to go on about my life, not realizing the near fatal mistake of disobedience I'd just committed. Two weeks later, at 11:11pm on June 19th, while sleeping in my bedroom, I would be awakened by gunfire. I had no idea that someone with an automatic assault rifle would riddle my bedroom with almost 15 shots; one of which, striking me in my leg; the others barely missing my son in the next room.

When I ignored God's warning, I had no idea what was headed my way, but God did. Which is why I sat in that hospital bed crying out to Him to forgive me for having not heeded His instructions. I had to repent because my disobedience almost cost me my life. I also had to repent for not believing in Him enough to actually do what He told me to. Because whether my mother refused or not, I still would have been in God's will because I would have been in a position to receive further direction.

An example of this can be found in Matthew 2:19-23, when an angel instructed Jesus' stepfather, Joseph, to leave Egypt and take baby Jesus to Israel. '**Now when Herod was dead… an angel…appeared in a dream to Joseph in Egypt, saying, "Arise, take the young Child and His mother, and go to the land of Israel, for those who sought the young Child's life are dead." Then he…took the young Child and His mother, and came into the land of Israel. But when he heard that Archelaus was reigning over Judea instead of his father Herod, he was afraid to go there. And being warned by God in a dream, he turned aside into the region of Galilee. And he came and dwelt in a city called Nazareth…"**

Joseph obeyed the angel's instruction and immediately left Egypt and headed for Israel. I, on the other hand, heard God tell me to leave, but instead, stayed in my Egypt. The fact that Joseph left Egypt, even if he didn't make it to Jerusalem, placed him in a position to receive further direction from the Lord which would eventually lead him to Nazareth. Had I have just *asked* my mother I would have been in Israel. Even if she told me that I couldn't stay, I would have been in a position to receive further direction. I missed my Nazareth out of fear of rejection and as a result, remained in a place where I almost lost my life.

Right there, in my uninsured hospital bed at Baylor Hospital in Dallas, I asked God to forgive me for having not done what He told me to. If I would have at least picked up the phone and did what Jesus told Peter to do, I could have avoided that entire situation. In Luke 5:4-6, Jesus told Peter, "Launch out into the deep and let down your nets for a catch." **But Simon answered and said to Him, "Master, we have toiled all night and caught nothing; nevertheless at Your word I will let down the net. And when they had done this, they caught a great number of fish...**' At first, Peter was like, "No sir, we do this for a living. We've already done that, and it didn't work." But after his doubtful observations he said, **nevertheless**. Had I been like Peter, I too would have told the Lord, "You know me, and my mother don't have a relationship. But **nevertheless at Your word I will**...at least call her." Peter obeyed and caught **a great number of fish.** Had I, she might have agreed. Instead, my life was almost taken. Am I saying that my mother was to blame? Absolutely not! She had nothing to do with my shooting. But looking back, perhaps if I'd asked, maybe God could have used it as an opportunity to mend our relationship. I'll never know.

Again, it was *at that point* that I came to repentance and *in that moment* my life changed, as it allowed me to receive God's mercy. It was as if once I asked Him to forgive me, He gave me a grace to get through that time. Throughout the whole ordeal, I didn't need much pain medication and my wounds healed fairly quickly. While the doctors and the x-rays said I had a broken bone, I felt nothing as I knew there was no way my bone could be broken because less than 48-hours after being admitted into the hospital, I was able to walk on crutches. Because I had no insurance, I only received two bedside, 10-minute rehab sessions and was quickly discharged after just four days. Thereafter, I had to rehab myself as I taught myself how to stand and walk again. But by His grace, God got me through it. I now know the only reason I was able to mentally recover from that near-fatal experience is because I admitted I was wrong. I acknowledged and confessed that I had sinned and was disobedient; to which, He was then able to help me through it. Not that He wouldn't if I didn't. But because I did, it went a lot smoother and quicker than it could have. That's because when you refuse to admit and confess your sins, you leave yourself at risk. Perhaps, this is the point where those 173 officers came.

Many of those officers may have seen and/or participated in something that cost someone their freedom and/or life. Their actions not only impacted those individuals but the family of those individuals. So, to have to carry the guilt of their wrongdoing on top of guilt of keeping the code of silence for a fellow officer's wrongdoing, had to have weighed heavily on their souls. They thought there was no way to avoid prison time, or they considered the ostracizing they would experience, so instead of doing the right thing, they instead chose death...at their own hands.

I'm quite sure those officers came to a point of repentance. I know because I refuse to believe that those men and women were not, at some point, good people. I refuse to believe that. And as such, there was a point when they wanted to do the right thing but didn't know how. The how would have involved repentance which would have involved having to incriminate other officers and/or spend time in prison. Prison, for an officer, is a death sentence. So, in their eyes, they'd rather take their own lives. And because they didn't know that they could have confessed their crimes and the Lord would have protected them perhaps the enemy came and told them the situation was hopeless and that they'd be better off killing themselves.

Had those officers known that they could confess their sins, repent, go to the proper authorities, and admit their part, God would have protected them in prison, and some, may not have had to do any time at all. Had those same officers repented, Jesus would have walked them through whatever trial, backlash, and humiliation they would have had to walk through, and many would be with their families today, sharing their testimony and helping other officers do the same. Don't think that's true? Then read up on Barabbas.

Barabbas was convicted of murdering a police officer and was on death row when he was pardoned. Yes, it was Barabbas, a repeat offender and murderer whom the community allowed to go free in the place of Jesus. Therefore, God's mercy abounds, even for corrupt cops. And this is in no way saying that those officers were corrupt. I use that example to prove the goodness and mercy of God. Unfortunately, the enemy talked those men and women out of their brave lives, and now a violent crime survivor is writing a book that may save other officers from doing the same. Therefore, It is my hope that their lives be not in vain. That their service be honored.

And that their stories are a reminder that repentance and mercy is available to all.

Repentance Defined

According to bestselling author, Pastor and Greek theologian, Dr. Rick Renner, repentance...

> "...is the Greek word *metanoeo*, which is a compound of the words *meta* and *nous*. The word *meta* means *to turn*, and the word *nous* is the word for *mind, intellect, will, frame of thinking, opinion,* or *one's general view of life*. When *meta* and *nous* are compounded, the new word depicts *a decision to completely change the way one thinks, lives, or behaves*." [3]

Therefore, repentance isn't about how **you** feel or explaining **your** actions; repentance requires a change in thought followed by a deliberate course of action thus resulting in changed behavior.

Real repentance will require you to change the way you think about the code of silence and will require you to do whatever is needed to correct your wrongdoing while also holding your fellow officers accountable. But in order to do so, we must first correct the way you think about *repentance, misconduct and the code* because if there's something in you that thinks it's okay to be silent about what you know is wrong, then that has to be corrected first. But it'll only happen when you change the way you think about repentance. So...

Pray this with me: Heavenly Father, please forgive me for thinking that just because I was legally justified, that I was justified with You. I ask You to forgive me for not even considering You during those times and for failing to repent and get it right with You. I will do better. In Jesus' name.

What Repentance Looks Like

So, now that you have a better understanding of what repentance is, the question now becomes: *What deliberate course of action can you take and what exactly does repentance look like, in your day-to-day?* Our answer to this can be found in the book of Luke.

In Luke 3 we find John the Baptist, a Preacher/Repentance Expert, holding a conference at a desert resort. As was his custom, John would teach attendees the importance of recognizing and acknowledging their sins. As opposed to being oblivious of their many offenses, he taught, that if they knew they'd wronged someone, they should ask, God and/or that person, for forgiveness. But he didn't leave it there. He then provided them with practical ways of how they could avoid committing the same offense in the future. After the conference, a few of the VIP attendees in various occupations...

> '...asked him, saying, "What shall we do [to enact this strategy corporately]?" [11] He answered and said..."He who has two [coats], let him give to him who has none; and he who has food, let him do likewise." [12] Then [the] tax collectors also came to be baptized, and [asked]..."[Great meeting John but]...what shall we do?" [13] And he said to them, "Collect no more than what is appointed for you."
> – Luke 3:10-13 (author paraphrase)

Soon thereafter, a few of the soldiers/officers that had been hired to do security for the event, asked him for a few tips on how they could incorporate repentance while on duty to which John recommended the following:

> **"Do not intimidate anyone or accuse falsely, and be content with your wages."**

Let's unpack that statement for a moment. The first suggestion John gave to the officers was...

1. **Do not intimidate.** Why did John's first recommendation have to do with intimidation? It's because your position comes with an automatic, innate authority of which If you don't remind yourself

that true power rests in meekness, you'll abuse it. So much so, that you'll try to intimidate those who don't quickly, and respectfully, acquiesce to your state-given authority. It should also be noted that John's statement, in the King James Version, says, "**Do violence to no man.**" Intimidation would be analogous to violence which would speak to excessive use of force but would also include 'physical or verbal harassment, physical or mental injury, property damage, inaction...and in some cases, death.' [4]

Remember, this chapter is about correction, which means there's something about the way you think about your state-given authority, and intimidation, which needs to be corrected. But what?

Answer the following questions in your Companion Journal and be as truthful as possible. Don't give the politically correct answer. Write what's in your heart.

(a) Why do you think citizens should immediately acquiesce to your state-given authority?
(b) Are you more upset that citizens aren't acknowledging your presence as a person or are you upset that they aren't acknowledging your state-given authority?
(c) Do you take their slow-to-do-it-ness as a sign of disrespect? (Y) (N) If so, does that disrespect warrant their failure to comply? (Y) (N)
(d) Is there a way to de-escalate a disrespectful interaction? (Y) (N) If so, how and if not, why?
(e) Should such an encounter be taken as disrespect or danger? (Y) (N)
(f) Does their slow-to-do-it-ness cause you to become fearful, and if so, why?
(g) Do you believe law enforcement agents should be fearless? (Y) (N)
(h) Have there been instances when you should have been fearless, but you used fear as an excuse to justify your actions? (Y) (N)

(i) Do you consider yourself a humble public servant? (Y) (N) If so, why or why not?
(j) In what ways do you think you can improve on not being intimidating?

There are officers who are qualified for the position, but are not qualified for the power.

Throughout the book, we will touch on your answers so expect some much-needed correction. Until then, let's get back to John's recommendations.

The second thing John recommended was...

2. **Do not accuse falsely.** That would mean that John was instructing these officers to not participate in acts of entrapment, planting evidence, coercing false confessions, making false arrests, falsely imprisoning, falsification of evidence, spoliation of evidence, perjury, and witness tampering. So, let's stop and ask the following questions...

    (a) What are your thoughts on entrapment?
    (b) If I were to surveil you at home, watch your every move, then orchestrate an opportunity for you to commit a crime, how would you feel about that?
    (c) What's the difference between you versus a citizen in your community?
    (d) Do you feel that certain people deserve to lose their freedom? (Y) (N) If so, what makes that person qualify?
    (e) What do you think justifies someone planting evidence?
    (f) Has someone ever led you to say something you didn't really mean? (Y) (N) How did it make you feel and what did you do?
    (g) What's the difference in someone leading you to say something you didn't mean and coercing false confessions?
    (h) Have you ever been accused of cheating or doing something that you did not do? (Y) (N)

(i) What's the difference in someone accusing you of something you did not do and false arrests and/or imprisonment?

Though the questions may be somewhat random, the purpose was to remind you that in every interaction you should always consider putting yourself in that person's shoes. This is one of the few times where selfishness is acceptable because within that selfishness is where you'll find selflessness. Your ability to consider how you would feel if in that situation will help correct your way of thinking.

Lastly, John recommended that the officers...

3. **Be content with [their] wages (salaries)**. When you went into law enforcement, you knew going in what the starting salary would be as well as your earning potential. When you first came onto the force, you made the decision that you'd be willing to take on this daily, dangerous assignment for the amount of pay that was being offered, and you agreed to be content with it. You agreed that the perks of the job, such as power, authority, and respect, outweighed the monetary compensation. Why then, now, do you feel entitled to more? Entitled, as in you should be able to legally extort, accept bribes, seize, and if need be, partake in a criminal enterprise?

Not only that, but why do you feel that because you are not being adequately compensated that you have the right to take it out on the people, or worse, your loved ones? These are questions you should seriously consider, and more importantly, pray about. To ensure that you do...

Pray this with me:

Heavenly Father, after ____ years on the force, I don't feel I am being properly compensated. Because I don't, I've _____
_____
_____
_____.

And for that, I ask You to please forgive me. Help me to be content with my salary and please show me what I need to do to get my desired salary. Whatever I have to do Heavenly Father, I am willing, and recognize that by doing so, this is an act of repentance. I thank You for forgiving me. In Jesus' name.

As you can see, these are three specific and practical ways in which you can proactively walk out repentance. Can you think of anymore? *(Please jot them in your Companion Journal)* Now let's settle once and for all if law enforcement is exempt from repentance.

Exempted from Repentance…or Not?

We touched on the fact that due to the nature of the profession; one could argue that law enforcement is exempt from repentance, but is that true? Let's go to God's Word for the answer.

Acts 16:16-34 says….

> **[16] Now it happened, as we went to prayer, that a certain slave girl possessed with a spirit of divination met us, who brought her masters much profit by fortune-telling. [17] This girl followed…us…saying, "These men are the servants of the Most High God, who proclaim to us the way of salvation." [18] And this she did for many days.**
>
> **But Paul, greatly annoyed, turned and said to the spirit, "I command you in the name of Jesus Christ to come out of her." And he [the spirit of divination] came out that very hour. [19] But when her masters saw that their hope of profit was gone, they seized Paul and Silas and dragged them into the marketplace to the authorities.**

²⁰ **And they brought them to the magistrates, and said, "These men, being Jews, exceedingly trouble our city; ²¹ and they teach customs which are not lawful for us, being Romans, to receive or observe." ²² Then the...magistrates... commanded them to be beaten with rods. ²³ And when they had laid many stripes on them, they threw them into prison, commanding the jailer to keep them securely. ²⁴ Having received such a charge, he put them into the inner prison and fastened their feet in the stocks.**

Here we find Paul and Silas, two ministers of the gospel, hosting a conference when they encounter a teenage influencer who decided to livestream their event to millions of her followers. Unfortunately, her posts led to a lot of negative press resulting in jail time for Paul and Silas. While jailed, Paul and Silas prayed and sang hymns, as the inmates listened. Their praise caused an earthquake which led to the cells being **'opened...and everyone's chains were loosed.'** When the guard saw **'the prison doors open, supposing the prisoners had fled, [he] drew his sword and was about to kill himself. ²⁸ But Paul called with a loud voice, saying, "Do yourself no harm, for we are all here." ²⁹ Then he called for a light, ran in, and fell down trembling before Paul and Silas. ³⁰ And he brought them out and said, "Sirs, what must I do to be saved?" ³¹ So they said, "Believe on the Lord Jesus Christ, and you will be saved, you and your household." ³² Then they spoke the word of the Lord to him and to all who were in his house. ³³ And he took them the same hour of the night and washed their stripes. And immediately he and all his family were baptized. ³⁴ Now when he had brought them into his house, he set food before them; and he rejoiced, having believed in God with all his household.'**

The jailer received salvation because of two prisoners, Paul, and Silas. The only way someone receives salvation is byway of repentance and by acknowledging that Jesus is the Christ, the Son of the Most High God. This LEO (law enforcement officer/official) did just that. When? When **he ran in, and fell down trembling before Paul and Silas**. When he asked, **"Sirs, what must I do to be saved?"** This was the moment this agent came to the point of repentance.

The miraculous thing about his conversion is that this officer saw the power of God. Not because of his upstanding morality but because of a prisoner's faith. Because Paul and Silas publicly expressed their faith in God's ability to keep and deliver them from such harsh conditions which was evidenced by praising God in the midnight hour, this officer not only experienced God's ability to deliver but was a beneficiary of a prisoner's prayer and was even used to be an answer to their prayer. His life was so impacted that he took Paul and Silas to his home, nursed their wounds, and his whole family repented and received eternal salvation. The person whose primary responsibility was to guard those who seemingly were ineligible for repentance, would be the very one who needed it.

Not only that, but one of the most popular phrases in Christian-dom was spoken by someone in law enforcement. The phrase, **'what must I do to be saved?"** was spoken by a jailer. Imagine that. Out of the mouth of a jailer came the words that so many Pastors refer to when they invite attendees to receive salvation.

On the flip side, an example of an officer needing to repent can be found with the officer convicted of keeping his knee on the neck of 46-year-old George Floyd for 9 minutes and 29 seconds. While watching the closing arguments, I realized that at any moment that officer could have publicly repented and said, "I did it. I knew I was wrong. I shouldn't have taken it that far. I apologize for taking his life and there is no need to continue this trial." Yet from May 25, 2020, the date of Mr. Floyd's death until April 20, 2021, the date he was convicted, he did not - not publicly anyway.

Since May 25th the nation has been waiting for some attrition, penance, or regret on his part but as of the time of this writing, we have not seen any. Not saying that he hasn't privately repented to God, but after everything the nation endured as a result of his action, you would think he would. As I watched the closing arguments, I noticed he kept his head down and his pen going. Though he was probably writing about the trial and making notes, each push of that pen told a different tale. I knew there were times when he wanted to cry out, so I prayed that when the weight of his actions become a bit much that he would use that same pen and write to God. I even asked God to give him the gift of repentance in his time of judgment. Then I realized that we were witnessing his judgment live. And though it was hard to watch, it has to be even harder to walk out. In that moment, he saw his life, career and failures play out in front of the American public. Yet there he sat - with his head down pushing his pen.

As I watched, I remember telling God, *"Oh Lord that he would just admit and repent so that he and WE as a nation could just all heal."* Yet he continued to push his pen, and we, as a nation, still have not healed from his sin. And this is an example of why officer repentance is needed.

Your actions don't just affect you they affect the nation. Though you live in a specific county and are duty bound to enforce the law within your designated municipality, your use-of-force decisions impact us all. In later chapters, particularly, *'The Objective Reasonableness Behind the Use-of-Fearful Force,'* you'll discover how that one incident has far-reaching effects. Prayerfully, you'll never find yourself in those situations, and if you have, then do your community, county, state, and nation a favor and publicly repent. Admit you were wrong so that we can all move on and stop using your badge as a position of exemption. Sorry, but it needed to be said. Let's continue.

*For a much-needed deeper dive into repentance, be sure to get your copy of *'The New 'It': 11 Whole Weeks of Nothing But 'It'* at stacisweet.com!

In our next example you'll discover the spiritual importance of repentance. In Numbers 31, we find Moses, God's general, and the children of Israel warring against the Midianites. After their victory, Moses notifies all military and law enforcement personnel to, "**...remain outside the camp seven days.**" The reason behind the notification will answer our exemption question.

Again, in Numbers 31, Moses said, "**...whoever has killed any person, and whoever has touched any slain [person must] purify yourselves...on the third day and on the seventh day. Purify every garment, everything made of leather, everything woven of goats' hair, and everything made of wood.**" Moses makes it clear, that because of the nature of your profession involves killing, you should set aside time and purify yourself because the blood of that person's life (i.e., the memory, the incident) is still upon your life and thus it is best that you spend quality time purifying yourself (your life) and your thoughts, by asking God for forgiveness and doing the self, soul, and spiritual care needed, to which these Moses' men complied. So, what's self-care, soul care and spirit care?

Self-Care

Self-care has to do with purifying your body. If you touched or came in contact with the deceased, God recommends that you purify your flesh. In fact, all throughout scripture, anytime anyone touched any dead thing and/or person, God required a time of purification. Purification as in removing *every garment, everything made of leather, everything woven of goats' hair, and everything made of wood*. Are you still wearing the same uniform that you wore when that life was taken? Do you still own the same pair of shoes? Are you still carrying the same service weapon? If so, you need to discard them immediately because this is a part of the purifying process. Not discard as in destroy evidence.

Soul Care

Soul care refers to your soul which consists of your mind, your will, and your emotions. During this time, you should take the time to think about the circumstances that surrounded the killing. Did you take a life because you were forced or was there something going on in your will that led you?

Soul care also involves taking the time needed to evaluate your emotions; to really think about where you were mentally before and during the incident. Were you upset or on edge before it happened? Could you have taken better control of the situation by taking control of your emotions? Now that's it's over, where are you emotionally? How do you feel? Have you allowed yourself to feel and/or grieve for the life that was taken, whether you were justified or not? Do you think that by grieving you're admitting fault, or do you believe grieving shows your humanity? All of these are things you need to consider.

But while we're on the subject it should also be noted that there are those of you who have salved your conscious by keeping certain cases 'under investigation.' Under investigation is a wonderful way to still do your job while others do nothing at all. And though this may make you feel as if you've done the right thing while the investigation continues to be ongoing, it does not make it right with God. Simply because while others slow walked justice, you, quite possibly contributed to others spending years of their life on probation, parole, mercilessly imprisoned, or worse, lost their lives while someone took their time about an investigation that never actually took place.

The thought of that is jarring. Not just for those who needed help, but for all parties involved in the investigative community. Your and/or their lives will be heavily impacted...spiritually. The miscarriage of justice is heavy...spiritually. Though everyone is seemingly fine - in the natural – soulishly and spiritually they are in danger because they have failed to repent. And not just in word but also in deed. So much so that they take the necessary steps to ensure the investigation is complete, thorough, and accurate.

That being said...

You need time to go before the Lord and ask Him to forgive you for your complicity, your willful ignorance, and the fact you haven't policed according to His standards.

Your fellow officers may be impressed with your fearlessness and quick temper, but God is not. And it is for that reason you should repent for your actions, purify your conscious, and seek the Lord for forgiveness. And when I say purify your conscious, I'm not saying purify it so that you can feel better. No, this is much heavier than your feelings.

I'm speaking of spending time in God's presence, byway of prayer and in His Word, to see if you were justified or if you acted criminally. You need to find out how you can manage those situations going forward and if there is anything you're supposed to do professionally and civilly to make it right. Because even though the officers mentioned in Numbers 31 were justified in their actions, it did not stop them from having to purify themselves - byway of repentance - and the same is true for you. Don't fool yourself into believing that you can take a life or do similarly damaging acts and it not affect you, because it does. Though you may not notice it psychologically, it is definitely causing catastrophic damage spiritually, and remember –you are a spirit. You have a soul, and you live in a body. You were **created in the image and likeness of God** which means just as God is a spirit, so are you which means what happened impacted your spirit more so than your head.

Spirit Care

Spirit care refers to your spirit. You are a spirit; you have a soul; and you live in a body. As a child of God, you were **created in the image and likeness of God** which means just as God is a spirit, so are you (Gen. 1:27, Jn. 4:24). The only difference is that your spirit is wrapped in a body. As a spirit, you must feed your spirit, like you would your body, and thus the Word of God is spirit food. During that time, you need to spend time, in the Word, feeding your spirit. But not only during that time. Because your life is on the line daily, you need to spend time in the Word everyday.

These particular officers were internationally known as mighty men of valor. Yet they humbled themselves to Moses' command to take the time to do the aforementioned. But why?

Because Moses was not only their general, but he was also a man of faith, and a man who prayed and had a relationship with God which resulted in him receiving God-given direction and orders for his men. Therefore, they knew his words were not his own, but God's, which meant they not only obeyed Moses, but more importantly God.

They could trust that their superior not only had their back legally but spiritually as well. You need leaders who care not only about your life, but your soul and your spirit. So much so, that they can recognize when you need time off. If you don't then know God does. And as such, you should seriously consider following His directive by taking the seven-day mandatory time off so that you too can comply with Moses' directive which again came directly from God. But again, why is this necessary?

Because these officers had taken lives in the line of duty. Not only were they active personnel but they were appointed to those positions by the Most High God. Therefore, they served both Moses and God, and this is a great stopping point to ask yourself: **Did you go into law enforcement of your own accord or were you appointed by God? Did God create you to enforce the laws or is this just a job with a great pension and benefits?** Though we'll go into that in greater detail later, it is a question you should ask yourself now because this will determine if you're willing to comply with God's orders.

But back to the point. Before these men ever stepped foot back into the precinct, their superior ordered them to get their soul and spirit in order. And though we've already touched on why this was important, it is also necessary to point out that though these men were in law enforcement, their actions not only required a legal remedy but a spiritual remedy as well. Legally, these officers could have been sued for wrongful death or charged with murder. And though both are serious, there is a spiritual remedy that we need to consider, and that spiritual remedy is atonement.

Atonement in Hebrew is kippur which means expiation. Expiation, as defined by Webster's 1828 Dictionary, is defined as, 'satisfaction or reparation made by giving an equivalent for an injury, or by doing or suffering that which is received in satisfaction for an offense or injury.' [5] During Moses' time, or in the Old Testament, sin offerings were required in order to pay or compensate for sin. In the case of taking a life, some, if not the family, will require and/or demand that some type of equal reparation occurs which may come in the form of termination, criminal charges, conviction, and in some instances, the death penalty. This, to some, is what should happen to those who kill. Yet the nature of your profession often does not. In fact, in most instances when a civilian is killed, it is often referred to as a justifiable homicide. Thus, making it seem as if no atonement, and/or repentance is required.

But as a Christian officer, you should know that...

Just because you're legally justified to take a life doesn't mean there will not be a spiritual penalty.

Just because something is real doesn't make it true and just because something is legal doesn't make it right in the eyes of God, and thus, as a Christian officer, you are still required to repent for your actions, whether justified or not.

Repent, in the sense that thankfully Jesus already atoned for every act of misconduct and/or homicide you'll ever commit. Not making light of the two, but the point is that atonement has already been made. The satisfactory equivalent for the injury and/or death you caused has already been paid for. The way you appropriate Christ's atonement is to repent. Without repentance, there can be no atonement which leaves you in spiritual danger. The only spiritual remedy is repentance and because you took a life, as was the case with the men of Moses' day, you need to take the time off to purify your spirit, soul, and body as well as repent before God the Father.

Another thing you need to know is that there is a certain grace, mercy and forgiveness that comes to those CREATED and CALLED into law enforcement. But such is not the case for all personnel. That grace, mercy, and forgiveness only applies to those who were created and called to that office. There are many that were never created to be in law enforcement which means the mercy and forgiveness afforded to those who are, may not be afforded to you. In which case, you need to seriously get before the Lord and make sure that you are in the right profession. But even if you are, no longer simply count killing as a part of the job. Yes, there are times when you're called to protect yourselves, and the lives of others. But for the most part, those times are JUSTIFIABLY few and far between as de-escalation should always be the action of choice. And should you have to take a life, you need to remember that you took more than a life, you caused a spirit to depart from this earth which means you need to spend time with God getting your spirit right afterward.

Again, just because your actions are legal and justified in the eyes of your profession and in the courts, in the eyes of God, you still need to repent and thus answers our question: **Does your profession exempt you from repentance?** As you just discovered, **according to scripture, it does not.**

May I Pray For You? Heavenly Father, I bring this badge wearing man or woman of God before You and ask that You give him/her the wherewithal, wisdom, direction, strength, assurance, and protection needed to repent for his/her silence, complicity and/or crime(s) he/she witnessed and/or committed. Just as the centurion boldly, openly, and publicly acknowledged what he knew, I ask that You help him/her do the same. Lord, I thank You for leading him/her to trustworthy, integrous personnel who'll walk beside him/her through the process. In Jesus' name.

SOURCES

1- "G3076 - lypeō - Strong's Greek Lexicon (KJV)."
2- Blue Letter Bible. Web. 11 Jun 2022.

2 - "Apology." *Merriam-Webster Dictionary*, Ninth New Collegiate Merriam-Webster. 1984.

3 - Renner, Dr. Rick. "Twelve Legions of Angels." *Rick Renner Ministries*, https://renner.org/article/twelve-legions-of-angels/. Accessed 8 July 2022.

4 - "Intimidation." *Merriam-Webster Dictionary*, Ninth New Collegiate Merriam-Webster. 1984.

5 - "Webster's Dictionary 1828 - Expiation." *Websters Dictionary 1828*.

Chapter 6: Objective Reasoning

We need to ensure that when faced with the same and/or a similar set of circumstances that your response is different which means our next order of business is to transition into your objective reasoning. Because it is that objectivity and that reasonableness that dictates your responses to citizens, affects the public's trust as well as determines the countless lives that have been lost and/or negatively impacted, from the lack thereof. Therefore, let's explore objective reasoning from a holistic view.

According to Wikipedia,

> "in United States criminal law...an objective standard of reasonableness requires the finder of fact to view the circumstances from the standpoint of a hypothetical reasonable person, absent the unique particular physical and psychological characteristics of" said person. [1]

In layman's terms, that would mean you have to view the situation and the person outside of his or her sex, race, sexual preference, aesthetic, national origin, age, political affiliation, financial status, religion, and/or disability. But the question for most reasonable people becomes, how can one see someone outside of the aforementioned? And furthermore, how does one identify a reasonable or right-thinking member of society? [2]

First, right-thinking has to do with what a person *thinks* is right or wrong AND what they *believe* is good or evil. Therefore, a reasonable person's beliefs would have to perfectly align with what's been established as the norm as far as the societal standard of morality is concerned. But how did morality make its way into the conversation?

Morality made its way into the conversation because laws are derived from a set standard of what has already been deemed right and wrong (i.e., morals) by members of congress. The penal code, in which you enforce, is determined by what's already been established as acceptable and unacceptable behavior. Therefore, a right-thinking and/or reasonable person's *thinking* and *beliefs* would mirror those already established. Thus, a reasonable person will respond in accordance with what has been legally established as acceptable or unacceptable (i.e., right or wrong) behavior, in any given situation, regardless to a person's sex, race, sexual preference, aesthetic, national origin, age, political affiliation, financial status, religion, and/or disability. And the reason they're able to do so is because they are guided and governed by either the societal standard of morality (i.e., the law) or a higher, more objective standard.

I mention this because if today's society says it's acceptable to shoot Black men, then as an enforcer of the societal standard, you will shoot Black men. If society says it's acceptable to detain law-abiding undocumented immigrants, then you, as an officer will detain them. And if society says it's acceptable to be more lenient to whites, then as an officer of the law when you see a mob of lawbreaking white citizens illegally enter the United States Capitol, you'll allow them to deface and destroy property while escorting them off hours later. But why would you do such a thing? Because society has established that these are acceptable norms and has been deemed what any reasonable person would do in any given situation. But it does bear to mention that lynching was considered acceptable in our modern-day society until the *Emmitt Till Antilynching Act* was passed and so was consensual and nonconsensual sexual activities with detainees by federal officers until the *Closing the Law Enforcement Consent Loophole Act* was passed in 2022.[3]

35 States That Allowed Consensual and Nonconsensual Sex With Detainees

Map source: Yahoo! [4]

Therefore, both society and its government officials thought it socially and morally acceptable to both lynch and sexually assault its citizens while simultaneously calling a siege on the Capitol everything but an insurrection in 2022. But I digress.

But let's go back to our original question of how does one look at circumstances and people outside of the aforementioned? One way to look at people outside of their sex, race, sexual preference, aesthetic, national origin, age, political affiliation, financial status, religion, and/or disability is to see them in accordance with the societal standard of normal and what it has deemed as:

1. The acceptable sex or gender
2. The acceptable race
3. An acceptable sexual preference
4. The preferred or acceptable aesthetic
5. The preferred or acceptable national origin
6. An acceptable age
7. The acceptable political affiliation
8. An acceptable financial status
9. The preferred and/or acceptable religion, and…
10. An acceptable disability

All of which can be evidenced *through our laws,* but we won't get into that today.

However, the second and most effective way to view any human being is *through the eyes of God.* And not to hyper-spiritualize the answer, but if said person, or in this instance – you, would view all people and every circumstance in light of scripture, you would then be applying a more objective standard.

Morality vs. Partiality

In the 1992 *People v. Serravo* case, "…the court wrote that a…moral wrong can be interpreted either by a purely personal and subjective standard of morality or by a societal and presumably more objective standard." [5]

Though the ruling lumped the societal standard and the more objective standard together, they are not synonymous because the 'more objective standard' can only be that of God's. But how can we be so sure? Because our constitution is founded upon the laws and principles found in the Bible. Therefore, what we consider normal, in Western culture, is primarily based upon the founding father's interpretation of scripture. And though the integrity of the Constitution is in question because of the founding fathers' moral failures, the Constitution still serves as the supreme law of the land*. But before we get into that more objective standard, let's be sure to clearly define objective so that we can better understand what a more objective standard would be.

Objective and Reasoning Defined

Objective, as defined by the Merriam-Webster Dictionary, is defined as, *'expressing or dealing with facts or conditions as perceived without distortion by personal feelings, prejudices, or interpretations.'* [6] Therefore, by definition, you'd have to put your personal feelings, preconceived judgments and opinions [7] aside and view every interaction *situationally*.

On the other hand, reasoning is defined as *'a fact, condition, or situation that makes it proper or appropriate to do something.'* [8] Hence, reasoning is more in line with the societal standard of morality because it determines what is proper and/or appropriate behavior. Therefore, when evaluating whether someone has broken the law, which in essence would be the same as committing 'a moral wrong', you're basing that assessment on the law or what has already been deemed right, wrong, acceptable/unacceptable, proper/improper, appropriate and/or inappropriate behavior. And as such, your assessment would then be derived from, '...a purely personal and subjective standard of morality or by a societal and presumably more objective standard." [9]

Again, that more objective standard of morality can only be that of a higher power. And not a higher power in the sense of the laws of nature, the laws of science, love, the flow of the universe, music and the arts, or humanity as a whole. Because in order for those powers to be higher or to apply to morality, they would each need to have a *universal* standard of morality within themselves. [10] Meaning, within the laws of nature, there would have to be a universally accepted standard of morality. Within the flow of the universe, there would have to be a standard of morality by which those within the universe agreeably flowed. And without arguing those points, it bears to reason that when it comes to both standards and morality, the more objective standard can only be that of God's. And not that I'm here to debate which god. But when I speak of God, I am speaking of the God of the Bible because it is in Him, in His kingdom, in His Son Jesus and in His Word where morality is clearly defined. Thus, helping you to better understand why He should be used as the benchmark for objective reasoning. And while some would argue the point, that's not our objective.

Our objective today is to ensure that, you, the finder of fact, as a child of the Most High God, go into every interaction objectively, reasonably and without fear or favor, remembering that in God there is no partiality or favoritism because it is in Him, "...where all men are created equal...[and]...are endowed by [Him as] their Creator with certain unalienable rights". [11]

Romans 2:11 and 12 put it this way. It says, **"...there is no partiality with God. For as many as have sinned without law will also perish without law, and as many as have sinned in the law will be judged by the law."** It should also be noted that James 2:9 says that **"if you [do] show partiality, you commit sin, and are convicted by the law..."** But before we move on, it is important that we briefly touch on the partiality mentioned in those verses because it is the partiality, or lack thereof, that will determine how objective you really are.

Partiality Defined

Partiality is an interesting word because in the Greek it means, 'to favor an individual or to be an accepter of a face.' Again, it's interesting because it proves that God doesn't favor a particular sex, race, national origin, or political party, and those who do, are in fact, committing a sin. It's similar to what happened to the Apostle Paul in Jerusalem. Paul had been wrongfully arrested and questioned her personal jurisdiction when he notified the sheriff's department of his citizenry, the officers notified their superiors that Paul was in fact a Roman citizen. Back then, Romans weren't permitted to arrest other Romans which meant the sheriff's department could possibly have been held liable for wrongfully detaining a fellow citizen.

Acts 22:27-29 reads, '**Then the commander came and said to him, "Tell me, are you a Roman?" He said, "Yes." ²⁸ The commander answered, "With a large sum I obtained this citizenship." And Paul said, "But I was born a citizen." ²⁹ Then immediately those who were about to examine him withdrew from him; and the commander was also afraid after he found out that he was a Roman, and because he had bound him.**' Why do I mention this? Because we see this type of partiality today in policing; only it's done under the guise of race. Typically, white officers are prone to ignore, excuse, or let other whites off with a warning, at best. Just like the Roman officers of Paul's time, officers today show partiality due in part to race. But who knew that showing favoritism or treating a particular demographic differently, was a sin? Who knew that things like:

1. Racial profiling
2. Entrapment
3. Needless pursuits and chases
4. Wrongfully accusing
5. Planting evidence [12]
6. Collecting and indexing genetic materials [13]
7. Coercing false confessions
8. Making false arrests [14]
9. False imprisonments
10. Falsifying evidence
11. Evidence spoliation
12. Perjury and Witness Tampering
13. Harsh sentencing [30]
14. Intimidation
15. Use excessive use of force [15]
16. Strip searching, and,
17. Participating in consensual/nonconsensual sex acts [16]...

Who knew that when you judge, police, or charge someone based upon sex, race, sexual preference, aesthetic, national origin, age, political affiliation, financial status, religion, and/or disability that it would be considered criminal and constitute as sin? Who knew that things like:

1. Christian Identity
2. Nationalism
3. Supremacy
4. Favoritism
5. Cronyism
6. Bribery
7. Selective Solidarity
8. Warnings in lieu of citations
9. Warnings in lieu of arrest
10. Citations in lieu of arrest
11. Ignoring or overlooking suspicious behavior
12. Failure to detain
13. Lesser charges, and,
14. Lighter sentencing...

For those of a certain sex, race, sexual preference, aesthetic, national origin, age, political affiliation, financial status, religion, and/or disability would constitute a sin? God did! In fact, James 2 shows us an excellent example of what partiality looks like. It reads,

> 'My brethren, do not hold the faith of our Lord Jesus Christ, the Lord of glory, with partiality. ²For if there should come into your assembly [precinct, community, or presence] a [white] man [or woman] with gold rings, in fine apparel, and there should also come in a poor [homeless, Black, or Latino] man in filthy clothes [or someone who you've racially profiled or that quite possibly fits the description of what a suspect looks like], ³and you pay attention to the one [white man or woman] wearing the fine clothes [who seems suspicious, is rude, disrespectful and may be breaking the law] and say to him [or her], "You sit here in a good place," [or ignore or give him/her a warning or lesser charge] and say to the poor man, "You stand there," [pull him over, stop and frisk him, conduct a search without cause or warrant, or harass him] or [tell him to],

"**Sit here at my footstool,**" [and illegally detain, falsely charge and over sentence him] **⁴ have you not shown partiality among yourselves, and become judges with evil thoughts?**' – James 2:1-4, author paraphrase

Those verses are an excellent example of both partiality and how objective reasoning works…apart from God. Two men came into the same room and were treated differently based upon factors that should have never been considered because the usher – or in your case, officer - failed to put his or her personal feelings aside. The interesting part is that the usher/officer worked in an environment where his or her behavior was acceptable. It was acceptable to treat the poor man harshly. Thus, living up to the societal standard of morality. What's interesting is that Proverbs says:

**Diverse weights and diverse measures,
they are both alike, an abomination to the LORD.**
– Proverbs 20:10

and…

**Diverse weights are an abomination to the Lord,
and dishonest scales are not good.**
– Proverbs 20:23

Remember earlier when I mentioned it was acceptable to shoot Black men, detain law abiding, undocumented immigrants while showing leniency to lawbreaking whites? At the time of this writing, 'of the 7,666 officers who killed people in the US between 2013 and 2019, only 25 were convicted while 74 were only charged.' [17] That means 98.7% were never charged criminally.[18] And during the Trump Administration (2016-2020), immigrant detentions and deportations rose nearly 40%. [19] Not to mention that from 2006 to 2018 there were only 158 officers charged with sexual assault, sexual battery, or unlawful sexual contact.[20] Conversely, white collar crime which 'refers to financially motivated, nonviolent or non-directly violent crimes committed by individuals, businesses and government professionals' which cost the US roughly…$300 and $660 billion' annually, only saw 4,727 prosecutions [21] in 2021 which is a 53.5% drop over a ten-year period. Thus, solidifying the societal standard of morality and demonstration of James 2:1-4 and Proverbs 20:10 in real-time.

So how can you avoid being like the partial usher/officer who failed to use objective reasoning the proper way? James 3:17 gives us the answer when it reads, "**...the wisdom that is from above is first pure, then peaceable, gentle, willing to yield, full of mercy and good fruits, without partiality and without hypocrisy.**" In order to objectively and reasonably serve and protect your community, you're going to need the wisdom of God for every interaction. By doing so, you can be assured you'll have peace, a pure perspective, a gentle approach, will be full of mercy, show no partiality or act hypocritically with the rich, the poor, and those you've mistakenly prejudged. If you do this, then your objectivity and reasonableness will align with how God sees and treats people, and thus, would mean you are using a more objective standard and thus would also be operating according to a biblical standard which by the way, always trumps those of your department, fellow officers and society's. And as such, as a Christian child of the Most High God, who also happens to work in law enforcement, would make you an enforcer of morals. I know that sounds strange but that is the essence of the law. The law being defined as, 'a rule of conduct or action prescribed or formally recognized as binding or enforced by a controlling authority.' [22] That controlling authority would be you.

Enforcers of Morality

According to the Stanford Encyclopedia of Philosophy, morality 'refers to a code of conduct that would be accepted by anyone who meets certain intellectual and volitional conditions, almost always including the condition of being rational.' [23] Rational in the sense of being reasonable. Therefore, by definition, the law and morality are interchangeably synonymous, and as such, would thus make you both an enforcer of the law and of morality.

Yes, you sir/ma'am are the keeper and enforcer of laws *and morality* which would by default, also make you the moral authority. Your state has given you legal authority to enforce the laws of the land. Those laws were established by both state and federal officials who determined what is right, wrong, acceptable, and unacceptable conduct, and thereafter codified that conduct into statutes and ordinances that we must follow, and you must enforce. Thus, when mentioned previously that your position comes with an automatic, innate authority, within said authority encompasses your ability to enforce the law while at the same time making you yourself a moral authority.

An example of this was during the January 6th Senate Hearings. In it, former Representative Liz Cheney (R-WY) asked 'retired United Stated Army lieutenant general' and former National Security Advisor [24], General Mike Flynn, this question. She asked: *"Do you believe the violence on January 6th was justified?"* General Flynn's counsel, Dhillon Law Group Partner, David Warrington, countered with the following: "Is that a *moral* question or are you asking a *legal* question?" Representative Cheney responded "Both!" to which General Flynn then chose to invoke his 5th amendment right. Clearly, this exchange solidifies the marriage between morality and the law because Mr. Warrington requested clarification of what appeared to be a straightforward question. [31] And thus, you can clearly understand why when an officer is accused of criminal activity, such as criminal or sexual misconduct, we the public make a huge deal out of it because we look to you to be the moral giants. Moral giants in the sense that your professional and private life should substantially surpass ours as citizens and notwithstanding those codified into law. Ethically speaking, '...[your] private life [should be] unsullied as an example to all and... [you should be behaving in [such] a manner that doesn't ...discredit [you] or...[your] agency', as cited in the International Association of Police Chiefs Law Enforcement Code of Ethics. [25] And though law enforcement is your occupation, in our eyes, we see you as not only moral giants but also as defenders of morality. Defender in the sense that because you are a moral giant operating in your role as a moral authority, we see you as someone empowered to defend and/or protect us from lawlessness and morally corrupt individuals, organizations, and/or corporations. We look to you to defend us from wrongdoers, protect us from violence while enforcing the rule of law. Therefore, when we see you in the line of duty, we are judging your performance based upon (1) *how well you apply the rule of law to all citizens,* regardless of sex, race, sexual preference, aesthetic, national origin, age, political affiliation, financial status, religion, and/or disability. We also want to be assured that (2) *your private morals align with what you expect from us professionally.* And more importantly, we are assessing (3) *how your impartial walk with God impacts all three.* Not only are we assessing your performance, but so is God. Colossians 3:22-25 says,

> "**Bondservants** [including police officers and all those in law enforcement], **obey in all things your masters according to the flesh** [which includes obeying superiors, departmental policy, local, state and federal laws], **not with eyeservice, as men-pleasers, but in sincerity of heart, fearing God** [not adhering to the code of silence and placing the brotherhood above Him]. [23] **And whatever you do** [as a law enforcement agent], **do it heartily, as to the Lord and not to men** [which include your superiors, fellow officers and the public], [24] **knowing that from the Lord you will receive the reward of the inheritance** [and not extortion, bribes, the seizure of possessions, or the profit of criminal drug and sex trafficking enterprises] ; **for you** [as a law enforcement agent] **serve the Lord Christ.** [25] **But he who does wrong** [shows partiality, favoritism, racially profiles, intimidates or is involved in any criminal activity, violates the law or adheres to the code of silence], **will be repaid for what he has** [or has not] **done,** [because] **there is no partiality** [no favoritism and no supremacism in God]." *Author emphasis/paraphrase*

As a defender of morality or one who took an oath to serve, protect and ensure that the conduct codified into law is enforced, you have a contractual and moral obligation to ensure that both your professional and private life mirrors, exemplifies, and far surpasses those within the community in which you serve.

And not so that you can power trip and throw your moral enforcement weight around but because we, as citizens and civilians of the community, need that example. And in case you're wondering, no; we are not expecting perfection from you. But we are expecting excellence, both on and off the clock.

However, in order to operate in moral excellence and be reasonably objective, you're going to have to put God first and get His wisdom. You're going to have to go into every interaction remembering that *you are a child of God first, and a law enforcement agent second.* Putting God first will allow you to see those circumstances and people objectively and from His point of view because remember: God sees the heart.

1 Samuel 16:7 says, **"For the Lord does not see as man sees; for man looks at the outward appearance, but the Lord looks at the heart."**

Officers who judge the outward appearance of a circumstance or person are often misled, simply because they are looking at that person's sex, race, sexual preference, aesthetic, national origin, age, political affiliation, financial status, religion, and/or disability. Their reasonableness is based upon the outward appearance which, in most cases, clouds or distorts their objectivity. As a law enforcing child of the Most High God, you have to put all those things aside and be led by your spirit which should be governed by the Holy Spirit. And if you are governed by the Holy Spirit, even when you enter into hostile and/or volatile situations, that according to the late Chief Justice William Rehnquist, requires you to make *'split-second judgments'* [26], you'll then be able to do so accurately without prejudice.

"
> *"... The calculus of reasonableness must embody allowance for the fact that police officers are often forced to make split-second judgments—in circumstances that are tense, uncertain and rapidly evolving..."* [27]
> - Chief Justice William Rehnquist

Chief Justice Rehnquist also cited, in the landmark excessive use of force Graham v. Connor case, in which, 'the objective reasonableness standard of the Fourth Amendment' [28] was challenged, that,

> '*...the test of reasonableness is not capable of precise definition or mechanical application.*' [29]

According to Justice Rehnquist, because of the split-second nature of your profession, there's no way to clearly define and/or mechanically apply reasonableness which only solidifies the importance of my earlier statement which is this: If you are governed by the Holy Spirit, even when you enter hostile and/or volatile situations in which split-second decisions must be made, because you are governed and led by the Holy Spirit, during those tense and uncertain situations, you can be assured that you are making a more objective decision because your objectivity and reasonableness are based upon what God sees, and nothing else.

But how can you be so sure? John 16:13 answers that question when it says,

> '**[The Spirit of truth]** will guide you into all truth **[surrounding that tense, uncertain, and rapidly evolving situation]**; for He **[the Spirit of truth]** will not speak **[to your spirit]** on His own authority, but whatever He **[the Spirit of truth]** hears **[from heaven about that tense, uncertain, and rapidly evolving situation]** He will speak **[to your spirit. Not in an audible voice but in your heart]**; and He will tell you things to come **[things that could happen, that you need to do in order to be secure while at the same time protecting others]**.'

The Spirit of truth will lead you and let you know what needs to be done in those crucial moments because the one thing you need during those times is the truth and not your preconceived judgments. You cannot go into any interaction with a prejudice. Your job requires you to have up-to-the-minute information about all parties, at all times. Therefore, to go into any given situation or approach anyone without up-to-the minute TRUTH, is both hazardous to your health and detrimental to the public's safety.

This is why it is important for you to keep the lines of communication between you and the Holy Spirit open at all times. You have to be open to receive wisdom and be led by the Spirit of truth, in order to safely, objectively, reasonably and accurately navigate the dangerous terrain of your profession. In order to do so, you are going to have to pray about ways to incorporate God into your duties. In fact, why don't you take a few minutes and jot a few ways in your Companion Journal. Be sure to check out the Immersion Learning portion in the Appendix for other ways. Until then, why don't you...

Pray this with me: Heavenly Father, I repent. I have not been objective or reasonable, both professionally and personally. I have let my personal feelings govern me and my prejudices navigate my enforcement decisions. I have been like the usher and have treated people unfairly while showing others favoritism. Lord, I need to also confess that I have not had the best morals and have behaved in ways that I shouldn't. Again, Heavenly Father, I repent, but not just in word but I ask You to teach me what is right, wrong, acceptable, unacceptable, proper, improper, appropriate and/or inappropriate behavior for myself personally and professionally, and please help me to enforce it accordingly. In Jesus' name.

Disclaimer: It is important to note that when I mention that the more objective standard can only be that of God's that you understand I am in no way saying that officers who don't serve the God of Abraham, Isaac, and Israel are not able to be reasonably objective. Not saying that at all. As a Christian, I can only attest to *my* God's Spirit and *His* ability to help *His* children do so. But again, this is in no way intended to offend those who serve other gods.

*For a more in-depth discussion about the founding fathers, faith, and the Constitution, be sure to get your copy of *'The Elephant in the Room: Hard Conversations About Faith and Race'* at stacisweet.com!

SOURCES

1 - Wikipedia contributors. "Subjective and objective standard of reasonableness." *Wikipedia, The Free Encyclopedia*. Wikipedia, The Free Encyclopedia, 6 Oct. 2021. Web. 5 Mar. 2022.

2 - Wikipedia contributors. "Reasonable person." *Wikipedia, The Free Encyclopedia*. Wikipedia, The Free Encyclopedia, 24 Jan. 2022. Web. 5 Mar. 2022.

3 - "Speier Celebrates Passage of Bipartisan Closing the Law Enforcement Consent Loophole Act." *Congresswoman Jackie Speier*, 9 Mar. 2022.

4 - "Congress Has Closed the Loophole That Allowed Federal Officers to Claim Sex with a Detainee Is Consensual." *Yahoo! News*, Yahoo!,

5, 9, 10- Wikipedia contributors. "People v. Serravo." *Wikipedia, The Free Encyclopedia*. Wikipedia, The Free Encyclopedia, 13 Nov. 2022. Web. 7 Dec. 2022.

6, 7 - "Objective." *Merriam-Webster Dictionary*, Ninth New Collegiate Merriam-Webster. 1984.

8 - "Reasoning." *Merriam-Webster Dictionary*, Ninth New Collegiate Merriam-Webster. 1984.

11 - "Declaration of Independence: A Transcription." *National Archives and Records Administration*, National Archives and Records Administration.

12 - Sanderlin, Lee O. "Granted Immunity, Former Baltimore Police Sergeant Admits to Decades Worth of Crimes." *Baltimore Sun*, 11 Apr. 2022,

13 - "NYPD Accused of Secretly Collecting DNA from Thousands of New Yorkers for 'Rogue' Database." *CBS News*, CBS Interactive, 22 Mar. 2022.

14 - Hall, Madison. "A Former Georgia Sheriff's Deputy Said He Wanted to Charge Black People with Felonies to Prevent Them from Voting, Court Documents Show." *Business Insider*, Business Insider, 29 Apr. 2021.

15 - Yancey-Bragg, N'dea. "Mississippi Police Chief Fired after Leaked Audio Captured Racist Rant." *USA Today*, Gannett Satellite Information Network, 23 July 2022.

16 - Mention, Bry'onna. "Cops Can No Longer Legally Have Sex with Detainees." *Essence*, Essence, 24 Mar. 2022.

17, 18, 20 - "Derek Chauvin Was Found Guilty – How Typical Is That of US Police Who Kill?" *The Guardian*, Guardian News and Media, 25 Apr. 2021.

19- "Ice Ero Immigration Arrests Climb Nearly 40%." *ICE*. US Immigration and Customs Enforcement.

21 - "20 Shocking White-Collar Crime Statistics [2022]: The State of White Collar Crime in the U.S." *Zippia*.

22 - "Law." *Merriam-Webster Dictionary*, Ninth New Collegiate Merriam-Webster. 1984.

23 - Gert, Bernard, and Joshua Gert. "The Definition of Morality." *Stanford Encyclopedia of Philosophy*, Stanford University, 8 Sept. 2020.

24 - Wikipedia contributors. "Michael Flynn." *Wikipedia, The Free Encyclopedia*. Wikipedia, The Free Encyclopedia, 20 Jun. 2022. Web. 29 Jun. 2022.

25 - "Law Enforcement Code of Ethics." *International Association of Chiefs of Police*.

26 – 29 - "Graham v. Connor, 490 U.S. 386 (1989)." *Justia Law*.

30 - Gerstein, Josh. "Police Killed His Friend and Blamed Him. He Got 65 Years. He Was 15." Mother Jones, 30 Mar. 2023, www.motherjones.com/criminal-justice/2023/03/police-killed-his-friend-and-blamed-him-he-got-65-years-he-was-15/.

31- Facebook. "Gen. Michael Flynn, former national security adviser to Donald Trump, testifies." Facebook, uploaded by MSNBC, 28 June 2022, www.facebook.com/watch/?v=326014709736733.

Chapter 7:
Lawful Orders, Probable Cause & Use of Force

With both terms, objective and reasoning clearly defined, with the understanding that you need both the wisdom of God as well as the Spirit of truth to do your job lawfully, morally, and in accordance with God's standard of morality, it's now time to delve into the legality of lawful orders, probable cause and the reasoning behind the use of force.

In a popular 2014 *Police Magazine* article entitled, *'Understanding Graham vs. Connor'*, a veteran police sergeant wrote that when,

> '...using the Graham standard, an officer must apply *constitutionally appropriate levels of force,* based on the unique circumstances of each case. The officer's force should be applied in the same basic way that an "objectively reasonable" officer would in the same circumstances.' [1]

Notice the Sergeant said, "...in the same basic way that an objectively reasonable officer would in the same circumstances." For the sake of continuity, the word 'another' should be added in order to understand the truth and the *standard* in which this former sergeant speaks. When you add the word another, his statement could now read, "...in the same basic way that [another] objectively reasonable officer would [apply constitutionally appropriate levels of force] in the same [set of] circumstances." At the outset, that statement seems harmless. However, it is the foundation of the landmark *Graham v. Connor* case and is the very crux of every use of force case and action, or lack thereof, nationwide today. How so?

Because as long as an officer uses excessive force and federal prosecutors choose not to bring charges because, yet *another* reasonably objective officer used the same amount of force and was never brought up on said charges, then excessive uses of force will continue to be the departmental and societal standard of codified morality (i.e., the law). To substantiate that claim, in a 2020 Syracuse University study entitled, *'Police Officers Rarely Charged for Excessive Use of Force in Federal Court'*, the study cites,

> "...that federal prosecutors rarely bring relevant criminal charges known as "deprivation of rights under the color of law" (18 U.S.C. 242) against law enforcement." [2]

It goes on to say that,

> "...In the first seven months of FY 2020, federal prosecutors filed § 242 charges in just 27 cases. In April 2020, just a month before the death of George Floyd sparked civil unrest, federal prosecutors did not report prosecuting a single case with § 242 as the lead charge." [3]

That means, prior to the worldwide coverage the George Floyd murder received starting May 25, 2020, nationwide, 27 **different** federal prosecutors determined 27 **different** times that 27 **different** officers ALL exercised objective reasonableness.

In the grand scheme of things, it's easy to believe that in a force of over 860,000 there were only **27 instances that warranted indictments.** With only .003% of § 242 charges brought against such a large police force, you could easily assume that police officers are amongst the nations' elite when it comes to being both objective and reasonable. However, what we need to consider is that those were **27 different civilians** who felt they had been excessively abused in addition to **27 different families** that will now have to live with the fact that not only did their police force fail to protect them but so did the federal courts.

Oftentimes, we tend to look at those **27 officers** statistically and merely refer to them as **27 bad apples.** But the thing we must also consider is that those are **27 different children of the Most High God** and **to Him**, each of them matter. But again, those were **27 different officers** who did what **another** reasonable officer would do **under the same circumstances** which lets us know that **the common denominator in all 27 cases is that each officer did what another officer would do which would be to use excessive force.** Thus, not only did these officers think it reasonable but so did **27 different precincts, 27 different superiors** as well as **27 different municipal, state, and federal courts.** To the naked eye those **27** appear to be only **27**; but again, in the grand scheme of things, they represent entire state and federal governments as well. Which yet again confirms that the societal standard for "constitutionally appropriate levels of force" is socially and governmentally acceptable. Why do I make that statement?

Because "most § 242 cases are first investigated by Federal Bureau of Investigation (FBI) agents or another federal agency, [and are] then referred to [the] U.S. attorneys within the Department of Justice who have discretion over whether to prosecute.' [4] That means that in addition to those **27 different officers**, within **27 different precincts** with **27 different superiors** whose cases were referred **27 different times** to **27 different offices within the Federal Bureau of Investigation**, that **27 different agents** and **27 different U.S. attorneys**, possibly **within 27 different states**, agreed that "constitutionally appropriate levels of force" is socially and governmentally acceptable.

And don't get me wrong. I'm not saying that there aren't times when force isn't needed. The problem is the quick accessibility to excessiveness has been the go-to option as opposed to de-escalation. Only within the law enforcement community is any type of force, excessive or not, acceptable which brings me to this question: *Do the majority of right-thinking Americans think use of force is acceptable?*

According to data collected in 2020 by the National Conference of State Legislators,

> "...at least 43 states have codified, at a minimum, some aspect of their use of force requirements [while some] ...41 states have statutes relating to law enforcement's use of deadly force. Most states require a violent felony to have been committed or a threat to human life to exist in order for law enforcement to legally use deadly force against a person." [5]

Therefore, in answering our question: *Do the majority of Americans think it's acceptable to use force? A*ccording to the data, the majority of right-thinking Americans – in at least 41 different states – think force is acceptable. [6] Therefore, not only do *police* think it's acceptable but so does the Federal Bureau of Investigation, the Department of Justice, as well as the majority of state legislators and the civilian populations in some 41 states.

Force Defined

So that we can better understand what the majority of our nation is in agreement with, let's legally define force, use of force, excessive and deadly force.

According to the Oxford Dictionary, the layman's term of *force* is defined as, 'strength or energy as an attribute of physical action or movement; coercion or compulsion, especially with the use or threat of violence.' [7]

As of July 2022, there is, 'no single, universally agreed-upon definition of use of force.' [8] The International Association of Chiefs of Police describes it as the "amount of effort required by police to compel compliance by an unwilling subject" [9] whereas the Police Data Initiative defines it as, '...the means of compelling compliance or overcoming resistance to an officer's command(s) in order to protect life or property or to take a person into custody'. [10] Keep 'an officer's command(s)' in mind.

Excessive force, as defined by Cornell's Law School's Legal Information Institute, states that excessive force is, 'force in excess of what a police officer reasonably believes is necessary.' [11]

Deadly force, in my state (Texas), is defined as, '...force that is intended or known by the actor to cause, or in the manner of its use or intended use is capable of causing, death or serious bodily injury.' [12]

Lawful Orders

With the aforementioned forces defined, the question we must now ask ourselves is: **What reasons could lead an officer to believe force is needed?** Again, the Police Data Initiative, 'a law enforcement community of...leading law enforcement agencies, technologists, and researchers' [13] gives us the answer within its use of force definition which again states,

'...The use of force can generally be defined as the means of compelling [civilian] compliance or overcoming resistance to an officer's command(s) in order to protect life or property or to take a person into custody.'

Notice the words, 'an officer's command(s).' Those three words, actually two, in my opinion, are the overarching problem within policing today and here's why.

Noncompliance or resistance to an officer's command(s), which is also commonly referred to as a 'lawful order,' is usually the reason why any type of force is used. Simply put, when a civilian fails to comply or resists a lawful order, officers are trained and are legally endowed to use force as a means to compel and/or overcome the resistance. So, what is a lawful order?

Lawful Order Defined

Much like there is not a 'single, universally agreed-upon definition of use of force,' the same holds true for a lawful order. On my many quests to find an official definition in the United States Code or on any government agency website and/or book, there was none. However, Cornell's Online Legal Information Institute offered the following:

> "Police powers are the fundamental ability of a government to enact laws to coerce its citizenry for the public good, although the term eludes an exact definition. The term does not directly relate to the common connotation of police as officers charged with maintaining public order, but rather to *broad governmental regulatory power.* Berman v. Parker, a 1954 U.S. Supreme Court case, stated that "[p]ublic safety, public health, morality, peace and quiet, law and order. . . are some of the more conspicuous examples of the traditional application of the police power"; while recognizing that "[a]n attempt to define [police power's] reach or trace its outer limits is fruitless."
>
> The division of police power in the United States is delineated in the Tenth Amendment, which states that *"[t]he powers not delegated to the United States by the Constitution, nor prohibited by it to the states, are reserved to the states respectively, or to the people."* That is, in the United States, the

federal government does not hold a general police power but may only act where the Constitution enumerates a power. *It is the states, then, who hold the general police power.* This is a central tenant to the system of federalism, which the U.S. Constitution embodies.

A state's regulatory power, therefore, is incredibly broad and is *limited predominantly by the state constitution,* powers which the federal government holds exclusively, the Takings Clause, and the incorporation of fundamental federal rights through the Fourteenth Amendment..." [14]

When you combine Cornell's definition with a comment written by former Yale Law School student, James Mooney, you'll soon discover the intersection between lawful orders, police power and state regulatory power.

Mr. Mooney writes,

"The power to give lawful orders rests on statutory or regulatory authority, depending on the jurisdiction. At least forty-four states, the District of Columbia, and the federal government make it a crime for civilians to disobey the lawful orders of officers. But these laws do not make it clear what lawful orders are. Legal scholarship has devoted little discussion to this question, despite the prevalence of lawful-order statutes." [15]

An example of this can be found in the state of New York. According to Mr. Mooney,

"New York criminalizes the failure to obey "any lawful order or direction of any police officer or flag person or other person duly empowered to regulate traffic," yet the statute does not define "lawful order or direction." [16]

This is a major problem with the use of lawful order because as mentioned earlier, *Closing the Law Enforcement Consent Loophole Act* wasn't enacted until March 2022 which means since the department's inception on May 23, 1845, the entire New York Police Department, which is the nation's oldest and largest police department[16a], could lawfully order and/or legally direct ANY motorist, at ANY time they deemed REASONABLE to engage in both outer and intercourse. This is disturbing because the entire NYPD had the authority to LEGALLY do so since its inception. Which means for 177 years it was LEGAL to have consensual and nonconsensual sex with detainees - in the 4th largest state in the United States of America. The disheartening part is that it took place under the careful watch of thirty-five presidents and administrations. **35.**

This is alarming because, 'the bill was initially introduced in 2018 after media reports emerged about a teenager in New York who was raped by two police officers while in their custody in the back of an unmarked police car. When the teen reported the rape, a loophole in New York state law allowed the officers to claim the sex was consensual despite the fact that the victim was handcuffed and under their control.' [17] Ironically, the only thing these two officers had to do to make this rape legal was to…give a lawful order. And though legislation passed that made their actions illegal, to date, 'New York's highest court has yet to establish a standard' [18] or provide a legal definition for a lawful order. And thus, we continue our slow approach to the intersection of lawful orders, policing power, and state regulatory power.

The Mystery Behind Lawful Orders

As we think about the fact, that prior to the *Consent Loophole Act*, legal officer rape laws existed in our nation for 177 years, which we should all wonder why? How is it possible that in 2022, when we have the technological wherewithal to have autonomous cars and have gone so far as to introduce H.R. 3711, the *'Safely Ensuring Lives Future Deployment and Research In Vehicle Evolution Act or the SELF DRIVE Act'* [19], to legislate 'highly automated vehicles' [20], yet we have not been so advantageous as to figure out and propose a simple definition of what a lawful order given by an officer who actually drives a patrol vehicle? **How is it that a lack of a judicial standard seems to allude elected government officials, empower police departments nationwide, while simultaneously remaining a point of contention for civilians?** As I prayed about the answer, God reminded me of a civil rights activist.

In a podcast he brilliantly explained that 'the United States doesn't just have one justice or legal system',[21] but, as he cited, there are more than 30,000 micro systems within the US Criminal Justice System. And therein lies both the complexity and the mysterious answer to what is a lawful order.

He stated that many mistakenly believe that the Criminal Justice System is one system but, "...it's not one system, with one set of rules, or one set of laws. [It's] 30,000 microsystems; [each] with their own set of rules and policies...that...has to be changed, independently, from the inside, out." And though he said that can be a daunting or insurmountable task, he believes it can be done one jail, one town, one law at a time, to which I wholeheartedly agree. Only I'll take it a step further and say that I believe in order to get this done expeditiously, it has to start from the inside. Meaning the inside of the spirits of the 30,000 state and local officials in charge of those 30,000 microsystems which is where you and I come in.

Though you, I, nor this legendary activist have the ability to change, overhaul or reform the entire Criminal Justice System, God, through this brilliant soul, and people like you and I can pray for and/or become one of those 30,000 leaders. And I believe that because you are reading this book, there is a call, gift, anointing, and/or grace on your life to change, overhaul, reform, and transform a part of those 30,000 microsystems. And though my part is small, my prayer is that you take what's in this book and share it within your microsystem while proactively making a difference in your community. With that in mind, let's find out how we can take 30,000 bite-sized chunks out of this elephant.

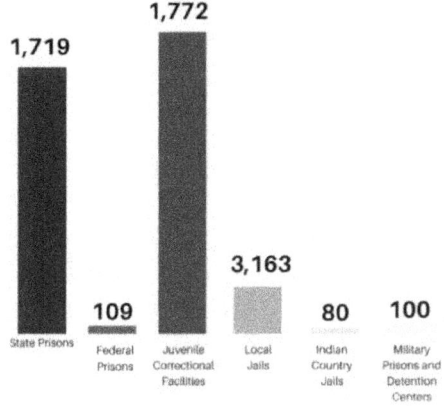

According to the podcast, to date, there are 1,719 state prisons, 109 federal prisons, 1,772 juvenile correctional facilities, 3,163 local jails, 80 Indian country jails, and 100 military prisons and detention centers. [22] That means, combined, there are approximately 7,000 jails and prisons in the US.

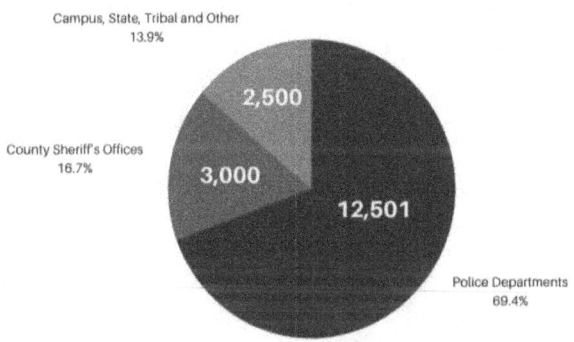

To date, there are verifiably 12,501 police departments, 3,000 county sheriff's offices, and 2,500 other police departments which include campus, state, tribal and other law enforcement agencies which means there is a combined total of 18,000 different law enforcement agencies nationwide. [23] Each department, office, and agency, whether federal, state, county and/or city operate in accordance with its *own* policies and statutes.

An example of this, he cited, can be found within the city of Atlanta. Though, "...cannabis in Georgia is illegal for recreational use... [it has been] decriminalized in the cities of Atlanta, Savannah, Macon, and a few others.' [24] "If a person were to take a dime bag of weed to the next city or county, which is still considered metro Atlanta, he or she would have broken the law." [25] Civilians are operating in and out of the many microsystems, just driving from one county to the next. Not state or country...county. But why did I include all that data?

To provide context and answer the mysterious question as to why our federal courts have failed to clearly define what a lawful order is and provide an explanation as to why they have not and/or cannot. The reason they cannot is because it varies...and that over 18,000 times, the number of police, sheriff's, campus, state, and other law enforcement agencies in the United States today.

But remember, 'the division of police power [which determines lawful orders] in the United States is delineated in the Tenth Amendment, which states that "[t]he powers not delegated to the United States by the Constitution, nor prohibited by it to the states, *are reserved to the states respectively,* or to the people" [26] which means, *"...the states...hold the general policing power."* [27] And thus explains why a lawful order cannot be clearly defined. The reason it cannot is because *each state has its own definition.* Consequently, there could very well be 50 different definitions of a lawful order in the United States today. Depending upon your state, your local government may have its own microsystem; each municipality with the ability to interpret and enforce its own lawful order or brand of justice. Thus, adding to the myriad of possible definitions.

But let's go back and review our original question which was: **What reasons could lead an officer to believe force is needed?** Again, we must remember the definition of use of force which is described as, "the means of compelling [civilian] compliance or overcoming resistance to an officer's command(s) in order to protect life or property or to take a person into custody." When a civilian resists, or fails to comply with a lawful order, officers are not only trained but are legally endowed to use force as a means to compel compliance. Because there is no clear-cut definition of what that order is, it remains a point of contention amongst civilians today and thus leads us back to our slow approach to the *intersection of lawful orders, policing power, and state regulatory power.* Each state has empowered its police force with the ability to give a lawful order and forcefully compel compliance. Unfortunately, this intersection is where Sandra Bland and a state trooper in Waller County, Texas met on July 10, 2015.

According to Reid J. Schar's 2015 article entitled, *"What Constitutes a 'Lawful Order"*, Schar writes...

> "After pulling [Ms.] Bland over for a failure to signal, [Trooper Encinia] asked her to extinguish her cigarette—a product she was legally entitled to smoke at the time of the stop. When [Ms.] Bland declined, the officer ordered her out of the vehicle. [Ms.] Bland refused this order as well, and an altercation ensued. Throughout the encounter, the officer repeated the following refrain: "I'm giving you a lawful order." But was the officer correct? Was the officer authorized, under law, to order [Ms.] Bland to extinguish her cigarette? And was the officer, upon [Ms.] Bland's refusal of that order...authorized to order [Ms.] Bland out of her vehicle?" [28]

Again, Trooper Encinia exercised his policing power regulated within the State of Texas and gave a lawful order to Ms. Bland to put out her cigarette, but what led him to believe force was needed at a traffic stop, with a woman, smoking a cigarette who was later arrested and found dead in her cell? Or what about the officer in the *Graham v. Connor* case, who misjudged the situation and assumed that a diabetic Black man had robbed a convenience store? Mr. Graham decided to leave the store due to the long line, which is what any reasonable diabetic person would do. He and a friend drove to another location where Mr. Graham could purchase the orange juice he'd left behind at the previous store, only to be given a lawful order to pull over by Officer Connor who made an objectively reasonable decision to use force against Mr. Graham. What led Officer Connor to believe that he was witnessing a robbery by a diabetic Black man?

In both instances, both officers believed force was necessary, but why? Our answer lies within the Fourth Amendment which states…

> The right of the people to be secure in their persons, houses, papers, and effects, against unreasonable searches and seizures, shall not be violated, and no warrants shall issue, but upon probable cause, supported by oath or affirmation, and particularly describing the place to be searched, and the persons or things to be seized.[29]

At first glance, it would appear that no mention is made of the use of force. Yet there is. It's hidden behind two words that motivated both Trooper Encinia and Officer Connor to respond with force. Those two words - probable cause.

Probable Cause Defined

Ballentine's Law Dictionary defines probable cause as, "a reasonable amount of suspicion, supported by circumstances sufficiently strong to justify a prudent and cautious person's belief that certain facts are probably true".[30] It is also widely held that its definition is mathematical in the sense of statistically speaking, it is *probable* that certain types of individuals have the propensity to display criminal behavior or commit certain crimes. And historically, this has been the problem with probable cause because if it is mathematical (i.e., based on statistics), then how were those probabilities derived?

For people of color, it is safe to assume that those probabilities derived from statistical stereotypes because statistically speaking, the rate of incarceration for Black Americans vs White Americans is 2,306 compared to 450 per 100,000+. The arrest rate for Black vs White Americans is 6,109 to 2,795 per 100,000[30a]. This lets us know that when officers encounter Black people, it is *statistically probable* that they will find cause which is unfortunate because according to the Library of Congress' Congressional Research Service, **there is no, "federal statutory provision relevant to the area [that] define[s] probable cause."**[31] Though Ballentine's provides a *definition*, its *definition* has no credence in a court of law because again, **there is no federal statute that clearly defines it.** And here's why.

Law.com, an industry-leading media platform specializing in legal publications, states that probable cause is subjective. [32] Meaning, the cause that led the officer to believe that it is possible and/or probable that something criminal is taking place is primarily dependent upon the officer's, 'personal feelings, tastes, or opinions', or as we just discussed, statistics. Since probable cause is subjective, it may explain why no federal statutory definition exists because how can lawmakers clearly define the subjectiveness of over 860,000 sworn police personnel?

In spite of the fact it has no statutory basis, probable cause is considered a standard in criminal law today. The irony of that statement is that it defies the definition of standard. Webster's 1828 Dictionary defines standard as, 'that which is established by sovereign power as a rule or measure by which others are to be adjusted.' [33] Though the definition is dated, when you think of a standard, this definition should come to mind. However, probable cause has no sovereign measure (i.e., federal statutory provision) by which states, or its officers, can look to as the benchmark, and this is important because the foundation of the Fourth Amendment is rooted in what an officer believes is possible and/or probable. Yet the very essence, footing, and underpinning of the amendment has no statutory basis. None. All the while, 12,501 police and 3,000 sheriff's departments, nationwide, continue to apply what the Sergeant referred to as the "Graham standard...[of]...constitutionally appropriate levels of force."

This means we have real-live LEOs enforcing a very real and written Fourth Amendment. Yet there is no federal statutory provision, state statute, or clear definition of the known facts, possible beliefs, and/or plausible reasons and/or examples of the required facts, beliefs, and/or reasons needed that would lead an officer to have probable cause, or give a lawful order, for that matter. How in 2022 is this possible? Because, again, it is *purely subjective*. It's only based on what that particular officer believes, which according to the law, is in accordance with what any right-thinking and/or reasonably objective person and/or officer would think.

Given the circumstances, probable cause, according to the Fourth Amendment, was to be used for the sole purpose of issuing warrants and/or conducting searches and seizures. Yet its use has spiraled beyond the corridors of the Fourth Amendment and has become the primary defense for all excessive and/or deadly force actions (i.e., cases) brought forth in the US. In fact, two cases determine the outcome of all "deprivation of rights under the color of law" (18 U.S.C. 242) a.k.a. § 242 charges brought against law enforcement today. Those cases being *Tennessee v. Garner* and *Graham v. Connor*.

Tennessee vs Garner

Unarmed Edward Garner was fatally shot by Officer Hymon while fleeing the scene of a home he'd allegedly burglarized. Though the officer gave Mr. Garner a lawful order, the officer still shot the 15-year-old as he continued to flee. According to Justia, 'a database for Supreme Court decisions,' [34] it stated that the primary holding for the Tennessee v. Garner case was that...

> "Under the Fourth Amendment of the U.S. Constitution, a police officer may use deadly force to prevent the escape of a fleeing suspect only if the officer has a good-faith belief that the suspect poses a significant threat of death or serious physical injury to the officer or others." [35]

The problem is that the Fourth Amendment does NOT say that "an officer may use deadly force to prevent the escape of a fleeing suspect only if the officer has a good-faith belief that the suspect poses a significant threat of death or serious physical injury to the officer or others." What the Fourth Amendment does speak to is probable cause, and within probable cause you'll find use of force and tucked away in the corner of use of force, you'll find deadly force. Again, the Fourth Amendment says...

> The right of the people to be secure in their persons, houses, papers, and effects, against unreasonable searches and seizures, shall not be violated, and no warrants shall issue, but upon probable cause, supported by oath or affirmation, and

particularly describing the place to be searched, and the persons or things to be seized.[36]

Therefore, within a term that has *no* federal statutory provision, state statute, or clear definition of the known facts, possible beliefs, and/or plausible reasons and/or examples of the required facts, beliefs, and/or reasons needed that would lead an officer to have probable cause - lies use of force, use of excessive force, and use of deadly force. And though we could discuss the objectiveness, or the reasonableness of what *Tennessee v. Garner* defines as a significant threat, the more critical issue here is that of escape.

Tennessee v. Garner went to trial in 1984. 1984 was the year the first PC was introduced, CD Rom was invented, and DNA fingerprinting was discovered; all of which limited policing and detective work. [37] Today, however, we have City surveillance cameras on every major highway and road; public and private security cameras and monitoring services for both the City and its civilians; vehicle registration information for every county; access to pinging and triangulation for every cell phone user; instant IP address locators for all devices; real-time location sharing abilities; satellite imagery, aerial photography, street maps, 360° interactive panoramic views of [every] street [in addition to] real-time [views of] traffic conditions [along with] route planning [capabilities whereas we can see every route someone could travel] by foot, car, bike, air and/or public transportation[38]. On top of that we have cameras and video recorders on most cell phones; sunglasses with video recording ability; multinational social media platforms with billions of registered users who voluntarily provide their name, date of birth, and/or DBA who also regularly record, upload video and data by the second. Yet an officer, who has high-level access to all of the aforementioned FEARS the escape of a fleeing suspect and thus, objectively decides that deadly force is needed.

Today, said use of deadly force is brought to trial under the "deprivation of rights under the color of law" statute 18 U.S.C. 242 and said case is determined by a Supreme Court ruling dating back to 1985; during a time in which the aforementioned technological options weren't readily available. Yet today's technically advanced officer isn't charged because of the lack of technology that existed in 1985, when *Tennessee v. Garner* was actually decided (it was argued in 1984). The ideology behind *Tennessee v. Garner* hasn't changed but the lifestyle and the technology of our nation and police force has. And as such, *certain*, not all, but *certain* laws involving fleeing suspects and use of deadly force, should be updated to reflect the current technology and the times in which we live.

Graham vs. Connor

In the *Graham v. Connor* case, Dethorne Graham was having an insulin reaction in which his friend took him to a store to purchase a bottle of juice. Because of the severity of his reaction, Mr. Graham thought it would be quicker to go to another store and upon his swift departure Officer Connor mistakenly reasoned that he'd just witnessed a robbery and decided to pull over the two gentlemen and thus commenced to using force, resulting in injury to Mr. Graham. Once it had been determined no crime had been committed, the officer brutally and disrespectfully dropped Mr. Graham home, thinking no harm no foul. And thus, we have *Graham v. Connor*.

The primary holding for the *Graham v. Connor* case was this:

> A claim of excessive force by law enforcement during an arrest, stop, or other seizure of an individual is subject to the objective reasonableness standard of the Fourth Amendment, rather than a substantive due process standard under the Fourteenth Amendment. [39]

The issue with this case is the previously discussed subjectiveness of the Fourth Amendment, in that the Fourth Amendment met the 'substantive due process' of the Fourteenth. The subjective-ness of a right-thinking officer collided with the clear and codified procedure of due process, only the objective reasonableness standard of the Fourth Amendment is again hidden within the undefined, non-provisional use of probable cause. And until our current lawmakers do what the late Chief Justice William Rehnquist admitted could not be done, which is to provide an assessment or a "precise definition" or at least an outline of a "mechanical application" of the reasonableness that's rooted in the Fourth Amendment, then the subjective application of both *Graham v. Connor* and the outdated use of *Tennessee v. Garner* will continue to be the standard.

So, let's review.

- There is not a 'single, universally agreed-upon definition of use of force.'
- Federal courts have not clearly defined lawful order.
- There is no, "federal statutory provision...[that] define[s] probable cause, yet it is considered a standard in criminal law."
- There is no federal statutory provision, state statute, or clear definition of the known facts, possible beliefs, and/or plausible reasons and/or examples of the required facts, beliefs, and or reasons needed that would lead an officer to have probable cause or give a lawful order.
- The Fourth Amendment cites probable cause, is held as the test of reasonableness while serving as the guidepost for constitutionally appropriate levels of force. Yet there's no "federal statutory provision...[that] define[s] probable cause" no is there "...a single, universally agreed-upon definition of use of force" nor have the federal courts clearly defined lawful order.
- *Tennessee v. Garner* is based on old policing methods and doesn't consider the technological advances of today.
- The subjective reasonableness of the Fourth Amendment overrode codified (written) procedure of due process that occurred in *Graham v. Connor*.
- .003% of officers nationwide are brought up on "deprivation of rights under the color of law" (i.e., 18 U.S.C. 242, § 242 charges) with 0% never being convicted.

SOURCES

1- Clark, Mark. "Understanding Graham v. Connor." *POLICE Magazine*, POLICE Magazine, 27 Oct. 2014.

2-4 -'*Police Officers Rarely Charged for Excessive Use of Force in Federal Court*',. Syracuse University.

5,6- L Vasquez, Amber Widgery. *Use of Force Standards*, National Conference of State Legislators, Nov. 2020.

7-"Force." *Oxford English Dictionary*, second edition (1989). Oxford University Press.

8, 10, 13-"Use of Force." *Police Data Initiative*, National Policing Institute, 21 Apr. 2017.

9 - "Use of Force." *International Association of Chiefs of Police*.

11 - "Excessive Force." *Legal Information Institute*, Cornell Legal Information Institute.

12 - *Penal Code Chapter 9. Justification Excluding Criminal Responsibility*, State of Texas.

14, 26, 27 - "Police Power." *Legal Information Institute*, Cornell Legal Information Institute.

15, 16 - Mooney, James. "The Power of Police Officers to Give 'Lawful Orders.'" *The Yale Law Journal - Home*, Yale University.

16a - Wikipedia contributors. "New York City Police Department." *Wikipedia, The Free Encyclopedia*. Wikipedia, The Free Encyclopedia, 24 Apr. 2022. Web. 30 Apr. 2022.

17 - "Speier Celebrates Passage of Bipartisan Closing the Law Enforcement Consent Loophole Act." *Congresswoman Jackie Speier*, 9 Mar. 2022.

18, 33 - "Webster's Dictionary 1828 - Standard." *Websters Dictionary 1828*,

19, 20 - "Text - H.R.3711 - 117th Congress (2021-2022): Self Drive Act."*Congress.gov*, Library of Congress.

21 – 23, 25 - King, Shaun. "Knowing How Its Built, So We Can Tear It Down." *The Break Down*, Apple Music, Oct. 2019.

24 - Wikipedia contributors. "Cannabis in Georgia (U.S. state)." *Wikipedia, The Free Encyclopedia*. Wikipedia, The Free Encyclopedia, 2 Apr. 2022. Web. 12 Jun. 2022.

28 - Schar, Reid J. "What Constitutes a 'Lawful Order'." *The Hill*, The Hill, 4 Feb. 2016.

29, 36 - "Fourth Amendment." *Legal Information Institute*, Cornell Legal Information Institute.

30 - *Handler, J. G. (1994). Ballentine's Law Dictionary (Legal Assistant ed.).* Albany: Delmar. p. 431.

30a - Published by Statista Research Department, and Dec 2. "People Shot to Death by U.S. Police, by Race 2022." *Statista*, 2 Dec. 2022.

31 - "Amdt4.1 Historical Background on Fourth Amendment." *Constitution Annotated Analysis and Interpretation of the Constitution*, Library of Congress.

32 - "Legal Dictionary - Law.com." *Law.com Legal Dictionary*, ALM Global,

34, 35, 39 - "Tennessee v. Garner, 471 U.S. 1 (1985)." *Justia Law*, Justia,

37 - "The Major Inventions of 1984 | Cass Art." *Cass Art*, Cass Art,

38 - Wikipedia contributors. "Google Maps." *Wikipedia, The Free Encyclopedia*. Wikipedia, The Free Encyclopedia, 24 Jun. 2022. Web. 6 Jul. 2022.

Chapter 8:
The Objective Reasonableness Behind the Use of Fearful Force

Contribution by Christian A. Sweet

With everything we just discovered, it's important that in the absence of having "no precise definition" nor description of the "mechanical application" of reasonableness or probable cause, that as followers of the Lord Jesus Christ, we, ourselves begin to analyze the reasoning behind why most right-thinking **Christian** officers' default to use-of-force rather than de-escalation. To do so, let's take a closer look at the nationwide use-of-force statistics for officers of all religions.

Use-of-Force Statistics

In 2021* 8,226 agencies, which represents 60% of total law enforcement today, submitted use-of-force data to the FBI's Uniform Crime Reporting Program for 2020*. That number dropped significantly in 2022** to 6,773 with just 40% of all federal, state, local, tribal, and college/university law enforcement agencies participating. [1] To give you a better idea of what that looks like, according to the same report, there are 860,000 sworn police employees in the US today which means in 2020, 516,000 officers were representative of the data submitted while 40% or 344,000 officers were unaccounted for. In 2021 that number rose to 516,000 officers which leaves the obvious question: Why? Why would only 40% of our nation's law enforcement personnel NOT submit use-of-force data to a ranking federal agency? Why would 60% of those who demand immediate compliance from their respective communities not be forthright and comply with the FBI? Perhaps there are pending § 242 cases, who knows. But let's take a closer look at the 2021* data, which to date, is the most current.

*Indicates the data submitted is for incidences that occurred during 2020.
** Indicates the data submitted is for incidences that occurred during 2021.

FBI Releases 2021 and First Quarter 2022 Statistics from the National Use-of-Force Data Collection

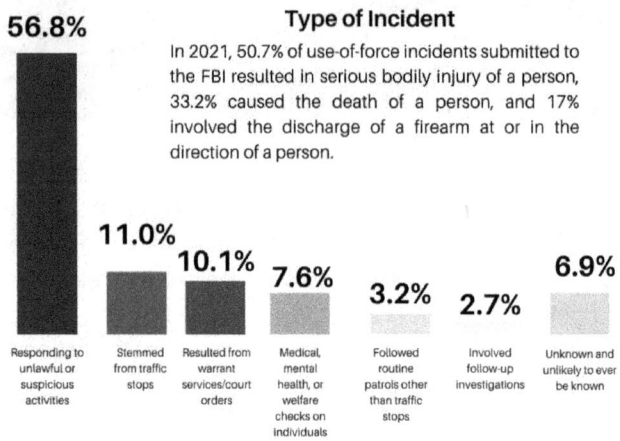

Type of Incident

In 2021, 50.7% of use-of-force incidents submitted to the FBI resulted in serious bodily injury of a person, 33.2% caused the death of a person, and 17% involved the discharge of a firearm at or in the direction of a person.

https://www.fbi.gov/news/press-releases/press-releases/fbi-releases-2021-and-first-quarter-2022-statistics-from-the-national-use-of-force-data-collection

As you can see, the highest percentage (56.8%) of use-of-force incidents were due in part to officers responding to unlawful or suspicious activities. Categorically unlawful and suspicious use-of-force incidents were grouped together, it would be interesting to know the percentages of those in which a clear violation of the law took place versus those in which suspicious or no crime occurred. Those statistics would be insightful as it would allow us to further classify the objective reasonableness that led to each officer's decision. That information would be particularly useful especially since the following data was not disclosed:

1) Total number of incidents per agency/department
2) Total number of incidents involving the same officer within the same department/agency
3) Total number of incidents involving the same officer nationwide
4) Race and gender of offending officer
5) Race and gender of individual in which force was used
6) Type of use-of-force incident cited per agency
7) Type of use-of-force incident cited per officer

- 100 -

All of the aforementioned are important because in July 2022, it was reported that a Lexington, Mississippi Police Chief boasted of justifiably killing **13 people** during his 16-year tenure [2] which means if and when § 242 charges were discussed, he was either found not guilty or was never charged **13 different times**. To give you a 360° view of what that looks like, that would mean on **13 different occasions** he quite possibly went before **13 different superiors** who reviewed each incident **13 different times**; thereafter, possibly undergoing **13 different federal investigations** which were referred **13 different times to the same U.S. attorneys' office** while **the Department of Justice reviewed this same officer's deadly force file 13 different times**. Yet in all **13 different incidences** it was determined that "constitutionally appropriate levels of force" were used on **13 different occasions** with **13 different individuals**.

Not only that but this same officer remained on the force, was promoted at least 5 different times and eventually went on to become the Chief of Police who would in turn become the superior to an entire police force and thus thereby become the superior who would then review other deadly force incidences. This is just the trajectory of **one** officer's repeated use of deadly force. And this is why it would be interesting to know the race and gender of the **13 different victims** in which **13 different federal officials** determined **13 different times** that "constitutionally appropriate levels of force" had been used by one officer because then we could further examine the probable cause and possibly get a better understanding of this former Police Chief's reasoning behind each incident. This is important because as a Police Chief, that reasoning would now influence not only an entire police department but an entire Mississippian town whose population is roughly 1,600, of which this officer quite possibly was responsible for killing .802% of its citizens.

*Please note: The image is for illustrative purposes only and is in no way intended to identify the gender, age, and/or race of the victim(s) or the US Attorney's and DOJ officials that reviewed each incident/case.

This is **one** state in **one** city in **one** county with **one** officer with **13** justifiable homicides during a **16-year** tenure which means he averaged at least **one homicide every 16 months**. To give you a panoramic view of what that looks like, in 2021, 50.7% of all use-of-force incidents submitted to the FBI resulted in serious bodily injury; 33.2% caused the death of a civilian, while 17% involved the discharge of a firearm at or in the direction of a civilian. That means approximately 261, 612* different officers (516,000 ÷ 50.7%) inflicted serious bodily injury and/or caused the death of a civilian which leads us to ask the following: *How many of those incidences were justifiably inflicted by the same officer and what has his or her professional trajectory been since?*

* Number could vary as no data for multiple incidences by same officer available.

On another note, take a look at the graph below.

Total Number of Federal, State, Local, Tribal, and College/University Law Enforcement Agencies (Reporting vs. Unreported)

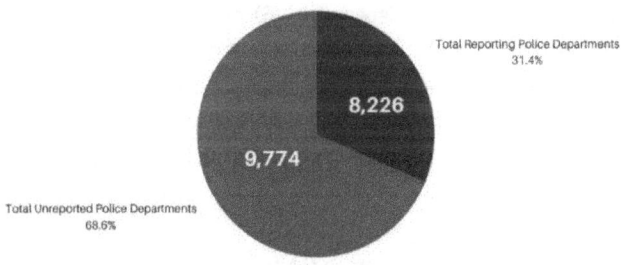

At the outset, the information can be deceiving as it would appear there were 8,226 *incidents* reported. However, 8,226 represents the number of agencies, not the number of total use-of-force incidents reported in 2021*. Though we don't know that number, we do know that *within* those 8,226 agencies there are at least 516,000 sworn police personnel and of those 516,000, at least 56.8% used use-of-force due to unlawful and/or suspicious activities; of which 50.7% resulted in serious bodily injury and/or death. It should also be noted that there are approximately 18,000 federal, state, local, tribal, and/or college/university law enforcement agencies which quite possibly means 9,774 or 54% of our nation's *state* and *local* law enforcement agencies failed to provide use-of-force data to the FEDERAL Bureau of Investigation which means it is highly probable those numbers will increase significantly. Think about that for a moment.

Out of 8,226 agencies, 50.7% of their use-of-force incidents resulted in serious bodily injury and/or death. **50.7%.** As someone in law enforcement, to you, that correlates to 50.7% of those within the law enforcement community. However, that same correlation is alarming to civilians as we associate that data to police brutality (i.e., police violence). And so, our question to you is...why?

Why would 8,226 reporting law enforcement agencies or approximately 261, 612 officers inflict serious bodily injury and/or cause death on those of whom they took an oath to protect and to serve?

Without unfairly answering that question by assuming that all reported incidents were unjustified, let's instead assume that a fair share was due to public and/or officer safety. But what other reasons could there be? A few that come to mind are (1) fear, (2) hate, (3) prejudice/racism, (4) pride, (5) demonstrated or perceived disrespect, (6) peer pressure, (7) entitlement, (8) control, (9) an outright abuse of power, (10) police training, (11) adherence to protocol, and/or (12) reenacting the historical roots of policing. Though one could assume, speculate, or rely on conjecture as to why, the most common reason or defense cited by most officers was fear, so let's tackle that one first.

Fear in Policing

Fear is defined as *'a painful emotion or passion excited by an expectation of evil, or the apprehension of impending danger.'* [3] This is an interesting definition because it substantiates probable cause. Probable cause states that, 'a reasonable amount of suspicion, supported by circumstances' would 'justify a prudent and cautious person's belief that certain facts' about the person and/or situation [were] 'probably true.' Therefore, it's **probably** safe to assume that those officers **probably** were suspicious and **probably** had an expectation of evil that led them to become apprehensive of some impending danger; either for themselves or for the public, at large. In fact, any officer on the force will tell you that fear comes with the job. And if you're in law enforcement, then any one of the following is **probably** a fear you face daily. Of which include but is not limited to...

1. Fear quotas won't be met.
2. Fear you won't be able to justify/explain your day-to-day activities.
3. Fear you weren't able to spot a crime-in-progress.
4. Fear you didn't do any crime fighting for the day.
5. Fear you'll be transferred to a different department.
6. Fear of being demoted.
7. Fear that you won't know what to do.
8. Fear for public safety.
9. Fear that citizens won't obey lawful orders.
10. Fear that the suspect could commit a crime.
11. Fear that the suspect is committing a crime.
12. Fear that someone is breaking a law.
13. Fear that law and order won't be kept.
14. Fear that law and order won't be restored.
15. Fear that someone will resist arrest.
16. Fear the suspect will flee.
17. Fear the fleeing suspect will escape.
18. Fear the suspect poses a significant threat of serious physical injury to the public.
19. Fear the suspect poses a significant threat of serious physical injury to other officers.
20. Fear the suspect poses a significant threat of serious physical injury to you.
21. Fear the suspect poses a significant threat of death to the public.
22. Fear the suspect poses a significant threat of death to other officers.
23. Fear the suspect poses a significant threat of death to you.
24. Fear someone has a weapon.

25. Fear someone has a deadly weapon.
26. Fear someone will use a weapon.
27. Fear someone will use a deadly weapon.
28. Fear that you won't be respected.
29. Fear that your peers don't respect you.
30. Fearing for your partner's safety.
31. Fearing your partner's criminal activities will be discovered.
32. Fear of not keeping the code of silence.
33. Fear of keeping the code of silence.
34. Fear you won't be backed up.
35. Fear of not knowing whether you'll make it home every day.

With all of the fearful scenarios just listed, as someone in law enforcement, how do you deal with all of that fear? Do you **(a)** live with/manage the fear, **(b)** medicate the fear byway of alcohol, prescribed meds, and/or use of illegal drugs, **(c)** overcompensate for the fear, or do you, **(d)** not deal with, suppress and/or ignore it?

Fear is Spiritual

As Christians, when it comes to fear, we are commanded to abide by 2 Timothy 1:7 which tells us that, **"…God has not given us a spirit of fear, but of power and of love and of a sound mind."** This verse lets us know that fear is a spirit. And though we won't get into a whole lot of spirituality per se, spirits are real.

To give you a better understanding, when Jesus notified the disciples of His impending crucifixion, He told them that He would leave them the Helper. John 16:7 says, "It is to your advantage that I go away; for if I do not go away, the Helper will not come to you; but if I depart, I will send Him to you." Him, or the Helper mentioned is the Holy Spirit.

Not only that, but Jesus tells us that, "…God is Spirit, and those who worship Him must worship in spirit and truth." And though your idea of spirits may be limited to what you've seen depicted in television or film, spirits are very real, and they can pressure and/or influence your behavior, and your policing decisions. To give you an example of a spiritual influence, go with me to Mark 5:1-9 which says,

¹ Then they came to the...country of the Gadarenes. ² And when [Jesus] had come out of the boat, immediately there met Him out of the tombs a man with an unclean spirit, ³ who had his dwelling among the tombs; and no one could bind him, not even with chains, ⁴ because he had often been bound with shackles and chains. And the chains had been pulled apart by him, and the shackles broken in pieces; neither could anyone tame him. ⁵ And always, night and day, he was in the mountains and in the tombs, crying out and cutting himself with stones.

⁶ When he saw Jesus from afar, he ran and worshiped Him. ⁷ And he cried out with a loud voice and said, "What have I to do with You, Jesus, Son of the Most High God? I implore You by God that You do not torment me." ⁸ For He said to him, "Come out of the man, unclean spirit!" ⁹ Then He asked him, "What is your name?" And he answered, saying, "My name is Legion; for we are many."

Notice this man lived in a cemetery (i.e., the tombs). The fact that this man lived in such conditions also lets us know (1) that he was homeless, and (2) that he was dealing with some type of mental illness; potentially the most dangerous type – Severe Paranoid Schizophrenia. On top of that, he'd had several run-ins with law enforcement because scripture lets us know that they couldn't, '...**bind him**...**because he'd often been bound with shackles and chains.**' Though there were times when he couldn't be restrained, there were also other times when he was placed into custody and was possibly charged but never received any substantial time. Nor had his numerous psychiatric in-patient stays proven successful, as clearly no psychiatrist or psychologist had been able to adequately treat and/or prescribe any medication that could '...**tame him.**' As a result, he was, '...**always, night and day...in the mountains and in the tombs, crying out and cutting himself with stones.**' So, not only was he a violent, mentally ill, homeless, repeat offender but he was also suicidal. Hence, the cutting of himself with stones. But how did he get that way? The answer to that lies within his answer. When Jesus asked him his name, he replied, **"My name is Legion; for we are many."**

Legion is significant because according to Greek theologian, Dr. Rick Renner, he writes that, "legion" is a military term that was taken from the Roman army. A legion denoted a group of at least 6,000 Roman soldiers, although the total number could be higher. [Therefore]...anytime [legion is used in the Bible] ...it always refers to at least 6,000 of something." [4]

That means this man was not only demon possessed but he had at least 6,000 demons both controlling and influencing his behavior. So much so, that they influenced him to live in a cemetery, engage in psychotic criminal behavior and ultimately talked him into multiple suicide attempts.

Again, the purpose of discussing this individual is to solely establish how spirits can influence behavior. And though we established that he was demon-possessed (demons are spirits), it should also be noted that Jesus clearly identified the *type* of spirit that possessed him.

> **⁸ For [Jesus] said to him,** "Come out of the man, unclean spirit!"

Thus, the type of spiritual influence that had possessed this man was an 'unclean' spiritual influence. Hence, his desire to be among dirt, death, and dead people.

Another example of how spirits influence behavior can be found in Mark 9. In verses 17-29 we find a father bringing his physically and developmentally challenged son to Jesus. It reads,

> **¹⁷ '...** "**Teacher, I brought You my son, who has a mute spirit. ¹⁸ And wherever it seizes him, it throws him down; he foams at the mouth, gnashes his teeth, and becomes rigid...²⁰ Then they brought [his son] to [Jesus]. And when he saw Him, immediately the spirit convulsed him, and he fell on the ground and wallowed, foaming at the mouth.**
>
> **²¹ So He asked his father,** "How long has this been happening to him?" **And he said, "From childhood. ²² And often he has thrown him both into the fire and into the water to destroy him. But if You can do anything, have compassion on us and help us."**
>
> **²³ Jesus said to him,** "If you can believe, all things are possible to him who believes." **²⁴ Immediately the father of**

> the child cried out and said with tears, "Lord, I believe; help my unbelief!" ²⁵ When Jesus saw that the people came running together, He rebuked the <u>unclean spirit</u>, saying to it, "<u>Deaf and dumb spirit</u>, I command you, come out of him and enter him no more!" ²⁶ Then <u>the spirit</u> cried out, convulsed him greatly, and came out of him. And he became as one dead, so that many said, "He is dead." ²⁷ But Jesus took him by the hand and lifted him up, and he arose.

Here we have a distraught father bringing his physically and developmentally challenged son to Jesus for deliverance. The thing we need to focus on is the boy's symptoms. Not only does the boy have seizures (**i.e., [the spirit] seizes him...[and] throws him down [and causes the boy to] foam at the mouth, gnash his teeth, and [he] becomes rigid**) but his father says his son also **has a mute spirit** to which Jesus identifies as a deaf and dumb spirit. Without going into a lot of detail, this boy clearly displays symptoms synonymous with several conditions, most notably, Autism. But again, notice that both the father and Jesus identified *the type of spirits* (unclean, muteness, deaf and dumb) that mirrored the boy's behavior which included uncleanness, difficulty speaking, deafness and intellectual challenges. Again, another example of how spirits influence behavior.

An example of how the spirit of fear works can be found in Matthew 14:22-27 which reads,

> ²² ...Jesus made His disciples get into the boat and go before Him to the other side... ²³ And when He had sent the multitudes away, He went up on the mountain by Himself to pray. Now when evening came, He was alone there. ²⁴ But the boat [which the disciples were on] was now in the middle of the sea, tossed by the waves, for the wind [speed was hurricane-like so] ...Jesus went to them, walking on the sea. ²⁶ And when the disciples saw Him walking on the sea, they were troubled, saying, "It is a ghost!" And they cried out for fear. ²⁷ But immediately Jesus spoke to them, saying, "Be of good cheer! It is I; do not be afraid."

Notice what the disciples did when they saw Jesus - **they cried out for fear.** Understandably there should have been some cause for alarm, especially since it is highly improbable for a human to walk on water. However, fear or the spirit of fear led these gentlemen to believe something that wasn't true. Fear caused the disciples to see Someone in a way that was neither real nor true. They thought Jesus was a ghost. Yet He was not. How often do we hear reports of officers "seeing" someone who looked suspicious, or even worse, officers who thought they "saw" a weapon. In most cases, what the officer thought he or she saw turned out to be false. Again, that spiritual influence (the spirit of fear) caused them to see someone or something in a way that wasn't true. Thus, another example of how the spirit of fear not only influences behavior but sight.

That being said, if you've ever stated, confessed, and/or reported that your actions were motivated *by fear,* then you, sir or ma'am, were pressured and/or were influenced by **the spirit of fear**. Thus, explaining your heightened suspicion, distrust, apprehension, anxiety, and/or extreme response. And though my intent was not to get into spirituality, it was important to firmly establish that what you experienced was spiritual. Whether it was fear you weren't being respected, fear for public safety or fear for your life; **all fear is spiritual**, and as such, you must remember that God didn't give you those thoughts or reactions (i.e., spirits). God has given you the spirit, **"…of power…love and of a sound mind."**

The Spirit of Power

"…for God has not given us a spirit of fear, but of power and of love and of a sound mind." – 2 Tim. 1:7

Power is defined as *'force, ability, abundance, might, and strength'* which lets us know that during those moments when you are fearful, Your Heavenly Father has ensured that the spirit of power is present as well. As a child of God, you can be assured that in the face of danger, you will have an abundant supply of supernatural power. You need only to be acutely aware that just as you were dispatched to render aide to the public, Your Heavenly Father has also dispatched the power of His angels to protect and to render assistance to you. In the same way you're familiar with the power and authority invested in you by the State, you should also know that Jesus has given you, "authority to trample on [those acting in a] serpent-like [manner or may be exhibiting scorpion-ish behaviors]". Not only that but He's also given you authority "over all the power of the enemy [foreign or domestic]." And even if by chance you do get into harm's way, "nothing [and no one] shall by any means hurt [you]."

In addition, you need to also become intimately acquainted with the power of His Word. Hebrews 1:1-4 says,

> "God, who at various times and in various ways spoke in time past to the fathers by the prophets, ²has in these last days spoken to us by His Son, whom He has appointed heir of all things, through whom also He made the worlds; ³who being the brightness of His glory and the express image of His person, and upholding all things by the word of His power, when He had by Himself purged our sins, sat down at the right hand of the Majesty on high, ⁴having become so much better than the angels, as He has by inheritance obtained a more excellent name than they."

Everything on the planet and in the heavenlies is upheld **by the word of God's power** which means you are going to have to get your words in alignment with His. And though we won't go into great detail, your words do have power. Proverbs 18:21 says, **'Death and life are in the power of the tongue, and those who love it will eat its fruit,'** which means what you say while you're on and off duty will determine the trajectory of your day, career, and life. You can speak words of death or words of life. It's totally up to you. But as we've already discussed, it is possible for a spirit to influence your speech. Remember when the disciples were afraid, they mistakenly called the Lord Jesus Christ a ghost!

There're some really great teachings on the power of words which I highly recommend. If you'd be so kind as to visit Charles Capps Ministries and search 'Words' for their entire catalog, and also Rhema Bible College, specifically under Brother Kenneth E. Hagin as both of these late, faith generals have provided extensive teachings on how words shape our lives.

And so that you won't think we've diverted from the subject of use-of-force, remember: the most cited defense for use-of-force cases was fear.

God has not given you the spirit of fear, but of power, and of love. You just learned about how fear influences you spiritually, and we just touched on the spirit of power and how the power of your words impacts the trajectory of your life, now let's do a deep dive into the spirit of love, what it looks like and how it influences your behavior.

SOURCES

1- "FBI Releases 2021 and First Quarter 2022 Statistics from the National Use-of-Force Data Collection." *FBI*, FBI, 31 May 2022.

2- Yancey-Bragg, N'dea. "Mississippi Police Chief Fired after Leaked Audio Captured Racist Rant." *USA Today*, Gannett Satellite Information Network, 23 July 2022.

3- "Webster's Dictionary 1828 - Fear." *Websters Dictionary 1828*.

4 - Renner, Dr. Rick. "Twelve Legions of Angels." *Rick Renner Ministries*, Accessed 8 July 2022.

Chapter 9: What's Love Got To Do With... Law Enforcement?

God's love is all throughout the Bible. 1 John 4:8 says, '**...for God is love**' while Matthew 22:37-39 records Jesus commanding us to, "...love the Lord our God with all our heart, with all our soul, and with all our mind. This is the first and great commandment. And the second is like it: [That we should] love our neighbor as ourself." Matthew 5:44 also tells us to, "...love our enemies, bless those who curse us, do good to those who hate us, and pray for those who spitefully use...and persecute us..." *As a sworn officer of the law,* you've taken an oath to protect and to serve. *As a child of God, who Himself is love*, you are commanded to love both your neighbor (i.e., the community in which you serve) and your enemy (i.e., lawbreakers). With that in mind, remember, "**God has not given you the spirit of fear but of power...love and of a sound mind.**" Therefore, when it comes to loving your community and lawbreakers, you don't have to be afraid; you need only to keep love at the forefront of your mind. But what is love and what does it have to do with policing? 1 Corinthians 13:4-8 lets us know exactly what love looks like when it says,

> ⁴ **Love suffers long and is kind; love does not envy; love does not parade itself, is not puffed up;** ⁵ **does not behave rudely, does not seek its own, is not provoked, thinks no evil;** ⁶ **does not rejoice in iniquity, but rejoices in the truth;** ⁷ **bears all things, believes all things, hopes all things, endures all things.** ⁸ **Love never fails.**

Let's dive right in and start with the first thing love does...

Love Suffers Long

While on duty you're going to have to suffer long. Suffer long as in being more patient and forgiving. How do you become more patient? By experiencing moments and people that try to provoke you to be impatient. Such as when you give a lawful order, you'll give the public an opportunity to process the order and if need be, explain the reason behind the order. That's what longsuffering looks like in action.

Another way to demonstrate longsuffering is to be 'slow to avenge wrongs.' Instead of being quick to pull over, quick to stop, and even quicker to lock up, practice longsuffering and patience.

> **'Let every [officer] be quick to hear [be a careful, thoughtful listener], slow to speak [a speaker of carefully chosen words and], slow to anger [patient, reflective, forgiving].'** - James 1:19 Amplified

Love is Kind

Ordinarily when you think of kindness, it's usually thought to be a feminine trait. Women are raised to be kind. Men are raised to be tough. However, the Bible lets us know that kindness is for us all. Proverbs 19:22 says, **'What is desired in a man is kindness, and a poor man is better than a liar.'** Notice the gender here is male. Yet Proverbs 31:26 says, **'She opens her mouth with wisdom, and on her tongue is the law of kindness.'** Though this particular verse refers to the virtuous woman, the kindness refers to the law which applies to both male and female. Consequently, on your tongue and out of your mouth, should be the same.

It should also be noted that the *Hebraic* definition of kindness refers to merciful speech. Surprisingly, the *Greek* definition of kind means 'to show oneself useful.' This is where your oath comes into play as kindness would be analogous to doing acts of service. So, whenever you're helping your community, you're not only being kind but in the eyes of God, you're also loving your neighbor.

This is another example of what love looks like and how it influences your policing behavior. The next example is…

Love Does Not Envy

Though this should go without saying, envy is something that may not be as forthright as you think. Envy is defined as 'to covet or to be jealous over'. Again, that's the obvious definition but it also means 'to be zealous or indignant.' Zealousness and indignance arise out of a person's beliefs which goes back to our discussion on objective reasoning where we discussed the anti-discrimination provision of the *Omnibus Crime Control and Safe Streets Act of 1968*, and *Title VI of the Civil Rights Acts of 1964*, which forbids discrimination on the basis of race, color, sex or national origin. If you have a *zeal* for your race or are *indignant* towards others who are not the same color, sex, or national origin, then you are being enviable. This also applies to those who don't share the same sexual preference or aesthetic as you. It also includes the disabled, non-Christians, and those who don't share the same political affiliation. If you police zealously or indignantly, then you sir/ma'am are in violation of the second New Testament commandment which is to love your neighbor as yourself.

Not only that but Jesus commanded you to, "…love your enemies, bless those who curse you, do good to those who hate you, and pray for those who spitefully use you and persecute you." That would include those who don't look like or share the same ideology, particularly those who support another political party or who also may support the Black Lives Matter and/or Defund the Police movements, respectively.

Love Does Not Parade Itself

This is probably another unexpected aspect of love that you haven't considered as someone in law enforcement because in your experience, who goes around parading? Parading, however, isn't a public procession, but parade in the sense of boasting. The Police Chief mentioned earlier was terminated because he paraded his justifiable homicides in a recorded rant. Other reports of officers bragging about punching handcuffed suspects, injuring suspects, along with other racist rants of killing Black and Brown people, is also at an all-time high. If polled, it would probably surprise us all if they were Christian; especially since such activities and boasting are considered an abomination. And though abomination is a strong word, the reason it's used is because such boasting is rooted in pride.

Proverbs 6:16-19 says,

> [16] **These six things the L**ORD **hates, yes, seven are an abomination to Him:** [17] **A proud look, a lying tongue, hands that shed innocent blood,** [18] **A heart that devises wicked plans, feet that are swift in running to evil,** [19] **A false witness who speaks lies, and one who sows discord among brethren.**

If you compare the entirety of those verses with the 516,000 officers, who reportedly inflicted serious bodily injury and/or death on those they encountered, it's probable that at least 50% acted abominably. Meaning, they either boasted about it, looked at someone in a proud way and abused their power; lied about why they stopped or interacted with someone; used deadly force, thus shedding innocent blood; devised a wicked plan to set someone up for a crime they didn't commit; submitted a false report, committed perjury, promulgated propaganda, spewed racist and/or controversial political views. Though seemingly unharmful, all are an abomination, as in disgusting, abhorrent, and even considered idolatry in the eyes of God. Yet many have bragged about it. So, what can be done? Several things. Of which include, stop entertaining, supporting and egging on those who do. When you see someone about to engage in an act that will bring future bragging rights, don't be silent, step in because this is what love does and this is how a loving Christian behaves.

The next example is...

Love Is Not Puffed Up

Puffed is defined as 'inflated or prideful' which we just discovered that something as simple as **'a proud look'** is abominable to God. Though similar to parading and boasting, policing in puffiness would be analogous to unnecessary traffic stops, stop-and-frisks, turning off body cameras, warrantless arrests and searches, confiscating property, false arrests and/or imprisonments, excessive uses of force, or forcing a detainee to have nonconsensual sex. All of which are abuses of power, and all of which are usually done out of pride or because an officer knows that most outcomes will result in no internal consequence and/or criminal indictment. Nevertheless, this is not the way a man or woman of God should police.

If anyone should have abused their power or acted puffy-ishly, it would have been Jesus. Yet when, '**...Pilate said to Him, "...Do You not know that I have power to crucify You, and power to release You?" Jesus answered,** "You could have no power at all against Me unless it had been given you from above..." ' (Jn. 19:10,11) Jesus could have taken out kings and kingdoms, yet He told His disciples, "...do you think that I cannot now pray to My Father, and He will provide Me with more than twelve legions of angels?" Scripture says that **'though He was rich, yet for our sakes He became poor, that you through His poverty might become rich.'** (2 Cor. 8:9) Wouldn't you walking in humility be an example of what this verse looks like in real time? To see you walking in meekness as opposed to seeing you travel at high rates of speed, making excessive stops, provoking various members of the public to anger while simultaneously forcing them to comply with unreasonable and unexplainable lawful orders would be refreshing. To see you quietly walking in your authority as opposed to throwing the weight of your badge around would be synonymous with you making yourself, '**...of no reputation, taking the form of a [civil] servant, and [serving] in the likeness of men.**' (Ph. 2:7) To see you de-escalate and not use force as opposed to you flexing and calling for twelve legions of backup would be a sight to see.

And allow me to say, on behalf of your community: "We get it! We know you have power and authority." But must we be constantly reminded? Because you are in a position of authority, you have the ability to change the narrative of how those in power move, treat and interact with their respective communities. Prayerfully you will.

Our next example of what love looks like is...

Love Does Not Behave Rudely

Rude has several definitions, of which include discourteous, offensive in manner or action, uncivilized and vulgar. As an officer of the law, you've probably witnessed fellow officers who are very impolite, offensive, and are downright vulgar, in word and in deed. Many of whom will defend themselves by saying that rudeness comes with the job. However, Ephesians 4:29-31 says, '**Let no corrupt word proceed out of your mouth, but what is good for necessary edification, that it may impart grace to the hearers. [30] And do not grieve the Holy Spirit of God, by whom you were sealed for the day of redemption. [31] Let all bitterness, wrath, anger, clamor, and evil speaking be put away from you, with all malice.**' Therefore, any type of rude, crude, or vulgar speech should not be coming out of your mouth. And though we could go into bitter, wrathful, angry, clamorous, and evil speech, the verse says love, '**...does not behave rudely;**' as in unbecoming, shapeless, or inelegant; all of which, define behavior.

Behavior Defined

Again, behavior is defined as 'unbecoming, shapeless, or inelegant.' [1] Unbecoming is defined as 'not according with the standards appropriate to one's position or condition of life.' [2] As an officer, you are held to a higher standard of behavior. That's a given. But as a child of the Most High God, you are held to the highest behavioral standards, of which we touched on in the chapter on *'Objective Reasoning,'* of which I encourage you to revisit in light of what you've learned so far about love. But in case you're not quite sure of those standards, the book of Galatians highlights both bad and godly behaviors. It reads,

> [19] **Now the works of the flesh** [poor behavior] **are evident, which are: adultery, fornication, uncleanness, lewdness,** [20] **idolatry, sorcery, hatred, contentions, jealousies, outbursts of wrath, selfish ambitions, dissensions, heresies,** [21] **envy, murders, drunkenness, revelries, and the like...** [22] **But the fruit of the Spirit** [godly behavior] **is love, joy, peace, longsuffering, kindness, goodness, faithfulness,** [23] **gentleness, self-control. Against such there is no law.**

This is what the public should experience every time it comes into contact with you.

Shapeless is an interesting word for behavior as it reminds me of a weightlifting belt. A weightlifting belt is worn as, **'a reminder to keep your spine in the correct position and can help maintain abdominal pressure to stabilize the spine during heavy lifting.'**[3] Your communication and interactions should have some shape to them so as to keep your spirit and demeanor in the correct posture so that you can maintain control over your emotions while under pressure during complex and/or split-second situations. Your adherence to God's commandment of love should shape your character and the way you police.

> **'But now...put off...anger, wrath, malice, blasphemy, [and] filthy language out of your mouth.'** – Col. 3:8

Our next example of what love looks like is...

Love Does Not Seek Its Own

This is a touchy one because it goes to the heart of planting evidence, coercing false confessions, falsification of evidence, spoliation of evidence, perjury, and witness tampering. All of which may be done to cover up a crime, guilt, and/or protect yourself (or a fellow officer) from termination and/or conviction. But as cited in scripture, love, **"...does not seek its own."** Meaning, it puts others first, which includes citizens of your community.

'By this we know love, because [Jesus] laid down His life for us. And we also ought to lay down our lives for the brethren.' - 1 John 3:16

Laying down doesn't necessarily have to do with putting your life in harm's way. But sir/ma'am, you can lay down your fear, your pride, and your ego, whenever you're tempted to set up, cover up, extort, fail to report and/or abide by the code of silence because this is how not seeking your own behaves.

Love Is Not Provoked

Provoked is defined as, 'to sharpen alongside, to exasperate.' [4] Exasperate as in to excite, inflame, enrage, irritate, or annoy. Therefore, when the Word says, '...**love is not provoked**,' it's speaking of YOU not allowing yourself to get enraged, inflamed, irritated, or annoyed...no matter what!

As human children of the Most High God, to us, that seems almost impossible; especially since we live on a dirty planet, in the midst of wicked spirits who do dreadful things through evil people. For us to even think that it's possible to NOT be provoked is an impossibility. But God would never tell us to do something that He hasn't given us the grace to do. Never. Therefore, if it is written that the second greatest commandment is we, "...love [our] neighbor as [our]self,' then that means even when they aren't being neighborly.

Jesus said to, "[44]...love your enemies, bless those who curse you, do good to those who hate you, and pray for those who spitefully use you and persecute you, [45] that you may be sons of your Father in heaven;

for He makes His sun rise on the evil and on the good, and sends rain on the just and on the unjust. ⁴⁶ For if you love those who love you, what reward have you?...⁴⁷ ...if you greet your brethren only, what do you do more than others? Do not even the tax collectors do so? ⁴⁸ Therefore you shall be perfect, just as your Father in heaven is perfect." - Matthew 5:44-48

As someone in law enforcement, the mere thought of loving a domestic and/or foreign enemy, being respectful to someone who's just disrespected you, or doing good to a suspect that has just committed a crime seems impossible. But again, Jesus would never tell you to do something that God hasn't already empowered you to do.

> "With men [it may seem] impossible, but not with God; for with God all things are possible." – Mark 10:27

Remember an officer of love doesn't allow himself to get enraged, inflamed, irritated, or annoyed. So how can you? Verse 48 gives us a clue when it says, **"Therefore you shall be perfect, just as your Father in heaven is perfect."** The thing about it is that Jesus isn't saying be perfect as in there won't be times when you can't help but be enraged. What he's saying here is you should be perfect as in mature. Therefore, when the Lord tells you to love a domestic and/or foreign enemy, be respectful to someone who's just disrespected you, or do something good for a suspect, what He's really telling you to do is to be mature in those situations. Jesus isn't telling you to not do your job. He's simply instructing you to be mature about it.

As adults, maturity isn't something that we usually discuss. Once we hit the legal age of 18, it's a given that we're now adulting. But it's been scientifically proven that the brain doesn't reach maturation until the age of 25 which means during those 7 years when we were recognized as adults, technically our brains still had some 28% or 7 years to go until science said that we were fully developed. The same is true in the spirit as 1 Corinthians 3:1-3 says, **'I [Paul]...could not speak to you as to spiritual people but as to carnal, as to babes in Christ. ² I fed you with milk and not with solid food; for until now you were not able to receive it, and even now you are still not able; ³ for you are still carnal. For where there are envy, strife, and divisions among you, are you not carnal and behaving like**

mere men?" It should be noted that Paul isn't speaking to literal children but adult men. What Paul was saying is that these adult men were acting, thinking, living, and behaving like babies. Not toddlers, children, or teens but infants, and depending upon the age of when these people gave their lives to Christ, he could very well be addressing adults in their mid-to-late '80s. Why do I mention this?

Because though you're a physical adult, it's possible that you're a spiritual babe. Depending on your walk with Christ, it is highly probable that you haven't matured to the point where you police maturely. Maturely, as in you don't throw the weight of your badge around like a child with a new toy. Mature as in you aren't so naïve as to look at a stranger and presume their guilt or innocence (i.e., racial profiling, favoritism). Mature as in you aren't easily angered so as to throw an adult temper tantrum when someone doesn't immediately comply with your lawful command. Mature as in you know how to de-escalate a threat. Mature as in you aren't a bully and your first instinct isn't always to use force. Overall, this is what love looks like because again, love is not provoked.

As children of God, we ofttimes provoke God to anger by our irreverence and disobedience. Yet God forgives and responds accordingly which means so should you. Not all interactions should result in some type of citation, arrest, and/or with some form of use-of-force action. There are times when you'll be provoked to go that route but like Your Heavenly Father, check your heart and see if this is an instance where mercy and maturation should be shown and sown.

Love Thinks No Evil

Though we've touched on this before, it does bear repeating. When you consider the fact that love thinks no evil, you have to begin to weigh God's thoughts and the way He thinks versus what you think, what the department allows, what is legal and what is constitutionally accepted when it comes to issues of sex, race, sexual preferences, a person's aesthetic, national origins, age, political affiliations, financial statuses, religions, and/or persons with disabilities. But why is that important? Because this is the brunt of police work.

The totality of your job involves serving and protecting people of both genders, 7 races, 23 sexual preferences, 5 political parties, 5 economic/income classes, 4,200 religions, and 8 main types of people with disabilities. With that being said, let's take a look at those statistics in action. Be sure to answer the following in your Companion Journal.

1. What are your beliefs when it comes to gender?
2. Where do you stand on racial issues?
3. What do you know about the 23 sexual preferences that exist today?
4. Where do stand when it comes to politics?
5. What do you think about the poor, lower-middle class, middle class, upper-middle class, and the wealthy?
6. What are your thoughts about people who worship other gods?
7. How do you feel about people with disabilities?

With those answers in mind, on paper, or in your Companion Journal, what does your department allow, the law, and the constitution stipulate? Please answer in your *Companion Journal*.

Now, let's find out...

What The Bible Thinks About Gender

The Book of Genesis is the book of beginnings, so it only makes sense that we begin our gender journey there. Go with me to Genesis 1:26, 27 which says, '**26 Then God said, "Let Us make man in Our image, according to Our likeness; let them have dominion over the fish of the sea, over the birds of the air, and over the cattle, over all the earth and over every creeping thing that creeps on the earth." 27 So God created man in His own image; in the image of God He created him; male and female He created them.'**

According to this verse, God **created man in His own image...male and female He created them.'** Thus, letting us know that there are only **two genders** according to the Bible.

What The Bible Thinks About Race

"Tell us, when will these things be? And what will be the sign of Your coming, and of the end of the age?" ⁴And Jesus answered and said to them: "Take heed that no one deceives you. ⁵For many will come in My name, saying, 'I am the Christ,' and will deceive many. ⁶And you will hear of wars and rumors of wars. See that you are not troubled; for all these things must come to pass, but the end is not yet. ⁷For nation will rise against nation, and kingdom against kingdom..." – Matthew 24:3-7

Nation, as it's used here, is ĕthnikŏs, which is where we get the word 'ethnic'. It's defined as *national* which is analogous to race and/or national origin. Jesus is telling us that in the last days there will be race wars. And though there are 7 main races in the earth today, Jesus settles the issue of race for us once and for all in the book of John.

In John 8 we find Him in discussion with the Jews whom He tells,

> "If God were your Father, you would love Me, for I proceeded forth and came from God He sent Me. ⁴³Why do you not understand My speech? Because you are not able to listen to My word. ⁴⁴You are of your father the devil, and the desires of your father you want to do. He was a murderer from the beginning, and does not stand in the truth, because there is no truth in him. When he speaks a lie, he speaks from his own resources, for he is a liar and the father of it."

What the Lord is telling us here is that there are two races on the earth. One, whose Father is God and the other, whose father is the devil. This answers racism simply. Though there may be cultural differences there are only two spiritual DNA's. That of God and that of the devil.

What The Bible Thinks About Sexual Preferences

Genesis 2:21-24 says, ²¹**And the LORD God caused a deep sleep to fall on Adam...and He took one of his ribs and...the rib which the LORD God had taken...He made into a woman, and...brought her to...man. ²³And Adam said: "This is now bone of my bones and flesh of my flesh; she shall be called Woman, because she was taken out of Man."**

²⁴ Therefore a man shall leave his father and mother and be joined to his wife, and they shall become one flesh.' The first reference to sex, *in the Bible*, can be found in the book of Genesis. In Genesis 2:21-24, we see God creating Eve, and her becoming Adam's wife. But there's no real mention of the act of sex until Genesis 4:1 which says, '**Adam knew Eve his wife, and she conceived and bore Cain...**' The word **knew**, as it's used here, means sex. We know this because the verse says, '**she conceived.**' Therefore, we know that the word *knew* is referencing sex because Eve had a child. But don't miss the point. Adam knew or had sex with his wife. Eve was married *before* she had sex. Therefore, sex was originally intended for a husband and a wife, and thus, according to scripture, we know that God does not support any type of premarital or extramarital sex - whether outer or inter, hetero or homo. And though neither God nor you may subscribe to alternative lifestyles, this should not affect the way you police. A person's sexual preference is between them and God, and thus, they should be afforded all of their civil rights.

What The Bible Thinks About the Poor, Lower-Middle Class, Middle Class, Upper-Middle Class and The Wealthy

Matthew 26:11 says, "**...For you have the poor with you always...**" Proverbs 17:5 says, '**He who mocks the poor reproaches his Maker; he who is glad at calamity will not go unpunished.**' When you discredit or disgrace someone and thereafter rejoice in the person's downfall, you will not go unpunished. "**He who oppresses the poor reproaches his Maker, but he who honors Him has mercy on the needy.**' (Pro. 14:31) Reproaching the poor is equivalent to reproaching God. This is because Jesus said, "...inasmuch as you did not do it to one of the least of these, you did not do it to Me.' (Mt 25:45) This would also apply to the lower-middle class as well.

As far as the *middle class, upper-middle class and the wealthy* are concerned, James 2:1-4 says, '**do not hold the faith of our Lord Jesus Christ, the Lord of glory, with partiality. ² For if there should come into your assembly a man with gold rings, in fine apparel, and there should also come in a poor man in filthy clothes, ³ and you pay attention to the one wearing the fine clothes and say to him, "You sit here in a good**

What The Bible Thinks About Race

"Tell us, when will these things be? And what will be the sign of Your coming, and of the end of the age?" [4] And Jesus answered and said to them: "Take heed that no one deceives you. [5] For many will come in My name, saying, 'I am the Christ,' and will deceive many. [6] And you will hear of wars and rumors of wars. See that you are not troubled; for all these things must come to pass, but the end is not yet. [7] For nation will rise against nation, and kingdom against kingdom..." – Matthew 24:3-7

Nation, as it's used here, is ĕthnikŏs, which is where we get the word 'ethnic'. It's defined as *national* which is analogous to race and/or national origin. Jesus is telling us that in the last days there will be race wars. And though there are 7 main races in the earth today, Jesus settles the issue of race for us once and for all in the book of John.

In John 8 we find Him in discussion with the Jews whom He tells,

"If God were your Father, you would love Me, for I proceeded forth and came from God He sent Me. [43] Why do you not understand My speech? Because you are not able to listen to My word. [44] You are of your father the devil, and the desires of your father you want to do. He was a murderer from the beginning, and does not stand in the truth, because there is no truth in him. When he speaks a lie, he speaks from his own resources, for he is a liar and the father of it."

What the Lord is telling us here is that there are two races on the earth. One, whose Father is God and the other, whose father is the devil. This answers racism simply. Though there may be cultural differences there are only two spiritual DNA's. That of God and that of the devil.

What The Bible Thinks About Sexual Preferences

Genesis 2:21-24 says, [21] And the LORD God caused a deep sleep to fall on Adam...and He took one of his ribs and...the rib which the LORD God had taken...He made into a woman, and...brought her to...man. [23] And Adam said: "This is now bone of my bones and flesh of my flesh; she shall be called Woman, because she was taken out of Man."

[24] **Therefore a man shall leave his father and mother and be joined to his wife, and they shall become one flesh.'** The first reference to sex, *in the Bible*, can be found in the book of Genesis. In Genesis 2:21-24, we see God creating Eve, and her becoming Adam's wife. But there's no real mention of the act of sex until Genesis 4:1 which says, **'Adam knew Eve his wife, and she conceived and bore Cain...'** The word **knew**, as it's used here, means sex. We know this because the verse says, **'she conceived.'** Therefore, we know that the word *knew* is referencing sex because Eve had a child. But don't miss the point. Adam knew or had sex with his wife. Eve was married *before* she had sex. Therefore, sex was originally intended for a husband and a wife, and thus, according to scripture, we know that God does not support any type of premarital or extramarital sex - whether outer or inter, hetero or homo. And though neither God nor you may subscribe to alternative lifestyles, this should not affect the way you police. A person's sexual preference is between them and God, and thus, they should be afforded all of their civil rights.

What The Bible Thinks About the Poor, Lower-Middle Class, Middle Class, Upper-Middle Class and The Wealthy

Matthew 26:11 says, "...For you have the poor with you always..." Proverbs 17:5 says, **'He who mocks the poor reproaches his Maker; he who is glad at calamity will not go unpunished.'** When you discredit or disgrace someone and thereafter rejoice in the person's downfall, you will not go unpunished. **"He who oppresses the poor reproaches his Maker, but he who honors Him has mercy on the needy.'** (Pro. 14:31) Reproaching the poor is equivalent to reproaching God. This is because Jesus said, "...inasmuch as you did not do it to one of the least of these, you did not do it to Me.' (Mt 25:45) This would also apply to the lower-middle class as well.

As far as the *middle class, upper-middle class and the wealthy* are concerned, James 2:1-4 says, **'do not hold the faith of our Lord Jesus Christ, the Lord of glory, with partiality. ² For if there should come into your assembly a man with gold rings, in fine apparel, and there should also come in a poor man in filthy clothes, ³ and you pay attention to the one wearing the fine clothes and say to him, "You sit here in a good** place," and say to the poor man, "You stand there," or, "Sit here at my footstool," ⁴have you not shown partiality among yourselves, and become judges with evil thoughts?

You should know that **"God is no respecter of persons: ³⁵But in every nation he that fears Him, and works righteousness, is accepted with Him.'** (Acts 10:34,35) This is the way you should think about the poor, lower-middle class, middle class, upper-middle class, and the wealthy.

What The Bible Thinks About Other Politics & Religions

We've already covered what the Bible thinks about other religions as this goes back to our discussion on *What The Bible Thinks About Race,* but it would do us some good to take Paul's approach. In Acts 17:16-34 we find the Apostle Paul in Athens where he discovered that...

> '...**the city was given over to idols. ¹⁷Therefore he reasoned in the synagogue with the Jews and with the Gentile worshipers, and in the marketplace daily with those who happened to be there. ¹⁸Then certain Epicurean and Stoic philosophers encountered him. And some said, "What does this babbler want to say?"**
>
> **Others said, "He seems to be a proclaimer of foreign gods," because he preached to them Jesus and the resurrection. ¹⁹And they took him and brought him to the Areopagus, saying, "May we know what this new doctrine is of which you speak? ²⁰For you are bringing some strange things to our ears. Therefore we want to know what these things mean"...²²Then Paul stood in the midst of the Areopagus and said, "Men of Athens, I perceive that in all things you are very religious; ²³for as I was passing through and considering the objects of your worship, I even found an altar with this inscription: TO THE UNKNOWN GOD. Therefore, the One whom you worship without knowing, Him I proclaim to you..."**

Paul then continues to explain the existence of God in a language they could both understand and appreciate to which, '...**some mocked, while** others said, "We will hear you again on this matter." ³³ So Paul departed from among them. ³⁴ However, some men joined him and believed...' Notice Paul didn't try to disprove their liberal, moderate, conservative, progressive, Libertarian, or socialist views. Neither did he try to convince them that because they worshipped idols that they were going to hell. He simply told them why he believed what he believed and allowed them to make a decision.

Though you might not agree with someone's political party or agenda, as a child of God, it is not your job to try to convince others they're wrong or to police in accordance with their disbelief. Your job is to live out what you believe.

What The Bible Thinks About the Disabled

All throughout the New Testament there are examples of Jesus healing the blind, lame, and the developmentally challenged. Therefore, the Bible not only supports the disabled but ensures they are treated fairly and equitably. Hence, the healing. Therefore, your treatment should mirror the Lord's.

What Do You Think About Diversity?

Our focus for the chapter is *'What Does Love Have To Do With Policing.'* The goal of the chapter was to focus on the fact that love thinks no evil and went into the fact that as a law enforcing child of God, you have to begin to weigh your Heavenly Father's thoughts and the way He thinks versus what you think, what the department allows, what is legal and what is constitutionally accepted when it comes to how you think about issues pertaining to sex, race, sexual preferences, a person's aesthetic, national origins, age, political affiliations, financial statuses, religions, and/or persons with disabilities.

We touched on that the totality of your job involves serving and protecting people of 2 genders, 7 races, 23 sexual orientations, 5 political parties, 5 economic/income classes, 4,200 religions, and 8 main types of people with disabilities. In light of what you've already learned and journaled, I want to walk you into what that statement might look like today. Because I'm from the lone star state of Texas, I'll start with the City of Dallas.

According to the Data USA's website, the City of Dallas is comprised of 41.9% Hispanic or Latino, 28.5% White and 24% Black or African American. Forty four percent speak a non-English language, while 80.9% are U.S. citizens. [5] Of those, 78% profess some sort of Christianity ranging from Protestantism, Catholicism, Mormonism, or Jehovah's Witness; while 4% are either Jewish, Muslim, Buddhist, Hindu, or another faith; with 18% readily identifying themselves as being atheist, agnostic, or nothing in particular. [6] The median income in Dallas is $50,627 while the poverty rate stands at 21.8%. [6a] That means of its 1.34 million citizens, 292,120 live below the national poverty rate of $12,490 for a household of one[7] with Dallas ranking 120 on the best and worst cities in the US for people with disabilities.[8] Not only that, but Dallas is '...also home to the 12th largest lesbian, gay, bisexual and transgender population in the United States.'[9]

Again, we'll use the City of Dallas as our example, but I challenge you to get a snapshot of your respective communities. With given the circumstances, and the fact that as an officer of love and the law that you are responsible for thinking no evil, how do fare on issues pertaining to...

- The Latino community, citizenship, immigration, and the border crises?
- What are your thoughts on the President, Republicans, and Democrats?
- What are your thoughts about wokeness, CRT (Critical Race Theory) or other conspiracy theories?
- What do you know about the plight of the black, Asian, and Indigenous communities?
- What are your thoughts about underemployment and unemployment?
- What do you think is the root cause of homelessness and what should be done about it?
- What are your thoughts about Islam, Buddhism, Hinduism, and Judaism, to name a few?
- Why does someone join and/or remain in a gang?
- What are your thoughts about anti-recidivism, and do you think redemption is possible?
- What are your thoughts about the LGTBQ community?

- What are your thoughts about the physically and MENTALLY disabled and mental health checks, de-escalation, and your ability to protect and to serve that population?
- What are your thoughts about treating and protecting older civilians?

Conversely, would you be able to report to...

- Someone of the opposite sex?
- A person of another color?
- A person of a different religion and/or political affiliation?
- Someone younger, and...
- How well do you take a 'no.'

These are all things you should not only think about but pray and study the Word for yourself as to how God thinks about all we've discussed. Be sure to complete the appropriate journaling exercise.

But while we're on the subject, let's apply all of what we've just learned to the recruiting process. In addition to assessing current personnel, let's take a look at the recruiting process and how those issues apply.

Diversity in Recruiting

Currently, in the City of Dallas, after an applicant has successfully completed a:

- Civil Service Written Test
- Preliminary Interview Questionnaire
- Physical Fitness Test
- Pre-Polygraph Questionnaire, and...
- Passed the Polygraph Exam

Applicants are required to go before the Interview Review Board. Because seasoned officers have the opportunity to ask the applicant questions directly, one would think the questions would be forthright and are designed to determine mental dexterity, honesty, and more importantly, evaluate the applicant's integrity. Because I've never gone through such a process, I had to rely on research for this portion of the book. That said, while watching an ABC Nightline report [10], which curtailed the murders of Botham Jean and Atatiana Jefferson, two upstanding black citizens that were murdered in their homes by officers Amber Guyger and Aaron Dean, respectively.

During the report, they showed actual footage of former Officer Dean's interview before the Tarrant County Interview Review Board. During the interview, he was asked what he liked about the job. His response, "I like the action, adventure stories that I was told about what the job seems to promise." This was disturbing and should have been an immediate red flag to the Board. For an interviewee to say that the reason he wanted to become an officer of the law was because of the action adventure the job promises says that (1) he was a bit immature, and (2) he didn't fully comprehend the gravity of the position nor the weight of the life and death responsibility it holds. Yet seasoned, supposedly mature officers thought it was the perfect response.

Next, he was asked something to the effect of how he would serve his community. His response, "I want to serve my fellow citizens in a very up close and personal way." That response was to be commended as this should have let the interviewer know that he was willing to serve. But there should have been a follow- up question. Something to the effect of define up close and how could you do this in a personable way? But in a final question he was asked "Will you be able to kill somebody if you have to?" Before we delve into his response, let's first look at the question a bit more just to ensure we understand its complexities.

He was asked *"Will you be able to kill somebody if you have to?"* Kill means *'to deprive of life, to put an end to.'* Therefore, the interviewer asked Mr. Dean if he would be able to deprive someone of the rest of their life, if necessary. I repeat, Mr. Dean was asked if he would be able to put an end to someone's life, if necessary. His response, *"No problem."* Though the Board thought it was the right answer, the Board was outrageously wrong for flippantly asking it. I mean think about it.

The fact that this question was posed in an interview - in 2017 - in the wake of an onslaught of police-involved shootings, lets us know that the problem with use-of-force begins with onboarding. Because if an applicant is asked

- in an interview - if they're willing to kill someone, the fact that he or she was asked the question, lets us know that there is some level of expectation that it may arise in the future. As an applicant, if Mr. Dean's response was, 'No problem', and he was later extended an offer, this sends a clear message that if and when a situation arises, given he was promised action and adventure in his interview, then when the unfortunate opportunity arose for him to put an end to Ms. Jefferson's life, then neither his employer, which just so happens to be a law enforcement agency backed by the state and federal government, would be surprised at his actions. Why? Because Mr. Dean clearly stated his intent. He clearly stated that he had no problem ending a Tarrant County citizens life, which would later be Atatiana Jefferson, at the time of his interview. His employer, the Tarrant County Police Department asked if he would kill. He answered truthfully, but unfortunately his answer came to pass. And though the question was appropriate, the fact that the recruiting officers did not follow up after his response clearly demonstrates the departments lack of sensitivity to conveying the weight and gravity of the position and the importance of saving the lives of the citizens it swore to protect, as opposed to killing them.

A better way to ask the question would be, in the event there was a life-threatening situation, what safeguards would you use to ensure that you did not have to kill one of our citizens? This allows officers to think pro-life as opposed to killing at will. And though this occurred in Tarrant County, it should also be noted that as of November 2022, the Dallas Police Department only requires cadets to obtain 10 course hours in multiculturalism and human relations. Ten. Conversely, the same department only requires 8 hours in professionalism and ethics. Eight. With that in mind remember 2 Timothy 2:15 says,

> **Study and be eager and do your utmost to present yourself to God approved (tested by trial), a workman who has no cause to be ashamed, correctly analyzing and accurately dividing [rightly handling and skillfully teaching] the Word of Truth.**

Though the laws within your state and your department may differ, you should spend as much time as you can, off the clock, continuously educating yourself in diverse subject matter so as to become as biblically astute as possible on issues that matter most to your respective communities so that you intuitively know how to engage and respond with those individuals because so much of what you do depends upon understanding how to engage with diverse populations. If you find out what God says – ahead of time - then during those high intensity moments, the Holy Spirit will bring to your remembrance the right response at the right time.

> "But the Helper, the Holy Spirit, whom the Father will send in My name, He will teach you all things, and bring to your remembrance all things that I said to you. Peace I leave with you, My peace I give to you; not as the world gives do I give to you. Let not your heart be troubled, neither let it be afraid." – John 14:26, 27

Be sure to summarize your thoughts, departmental policy, the law, and the constitution VERSUS what the Bible says in your Companion Journal. But before you do, consider this.

Matthew 27:9 says, **"Then was fulfilled what was spoken by Jeremiah the prophet, saying, "And they took the thirty pieces of silver, the value of Him who was priced, whom they of the children of Israel priced."** This verse is speaking of the amount Judas was paid by the chief priests to betray Jesus. My question for you is why would those who were supposed to know the law and the prophets, want to kill the One in which the prophets spoke of? The answer to that question is that the chief priests, Pharisees, Sadducees, and the scribes – knew the law, but they really didn't know the prophets. In other words, they didn't see the prophets as men. They merely read the Torah and the 17 books of the prophets as history. This is how you should see God's Word. Not merely read it as history or as some good book but read the words, research the historical data, find out about the back stories and ask yourself – and God- questions about the writers and those in which they wrote.

For example, people tend to think that Jesus walked around healing people while being bullied and criticized by the Pharisees all time. But when you read the gospels closely, you'll discover that Jesus was very direct and forthright with them 95% of the time. Though they made it their duty to point out every flaw or behavior that they thought didn't line up with the law, the Lord would check and correct them the majority of the time. Why is this significant? Because it helps you to see the Lord's humanity; to see Him as a Man, who had feelings, and responded in ways similar to your own. But how was I able to know that about the Lord? The same way I am suggesting that you do and that's to read the scriptures for the purpose of getting to know as much about the writers, the backstories, and more importantly, about the Lord and our Heavenly Father as possible. The more you want to know, the more God will reveal, and thus you continue to update and educate yourself, scripturally. Because again, though your department's standard of diversity may differ, you should spend as much time as you can, off the clock, continuously educating yourself so as to become biblically astute on issues that matter most to God, and to your respective communities.

But getting back to our discussion about use-of-force, the fear defense and how God has not given you the spirit of fear, but of power, and of love, you've learned that fear is a spiritual influence. We've also been discussing the spirit of love, what it looks like and how it influences your behavior. We took a side journey on **"…love thinks no evil,"** so as to ensure your thoughts were in line with what the Bible says, so let's wrap up our love study. Next one up…

Love Does Not Rejoice In Iniquity, But Rejoices In The Truth

Iniquity means injustice. Therefore, 1 Corinthians 13:6 could now read, **"love does not rejoice in injustice, but rejoices in the truth."** I'll not take for granted that because you work for law enforcement or within the criminal JUSTICE system that you know what injustice means. Not biblical injustice anyway so as to ensure you have a biblical point of view, let's look at the Old Covenant. In Leviticus 19:15 the LORD tells the children of Israel, **"'You shall do no injustice in judgment. You shall not be partial to the poor, nor honor the person of the mighty. In righteousness you shall judge your neighbor."**

Deuteronomy 32:4 says, **"[God] is the Rock, His work is perfect; for all His ways are justice, a God of truth and without injustice; righteous and upright is He.'** Therefore, injustice is when you judge prematurely (i.e., are prejudice), practice unfairness, promote inequity, and avoid the truth. Every interaction should be done fairly, equitably, and in truth, emphasis on the truth.

Love Bears All Things

Bear is an interesting word. In the Common English Bible, 1 Corinthians 13:7 reads, '**...Love puts up with all things.**' The Easy-To-Read version says, '**Love never gives up on people.**' While the New Life Translation puts it this way, "**Love takes everything that comes without giving up.**" Can you imagine taking this approach to policing? Putting up with those within your respective community who don't have it all together yet. Not giving up on repeat offenders. Giving people second, third, and if need be, several chances. This is what this verse looks like.

Love Believes, Hopes, and Endures All Things

Understanding that there may be some safety concerns with this verse but just remember, it's not so much as believing everything everyone says as it's being open to believe the best in everyone first. It's more about not making a false assumption, racially profiling, or instantly assuming someone who looks like you won't break the law. It's policing in hope.

For we were saved in this hope, but hope that is seen is not hope; for why does one still hope for what he sees? [25] But if we hope for what we do not see, we eagerly wait for it with perseverance.

What would happen if you actually believed the best for the lawbreakers in your community? What if you actually went out of your way to connect them to services, programs, mentors, and opportunities INSTEAD of making an arrest? Am I saying you should do this all the time? Absolutely not! But even in those instances where corrective action has to be taken why not follow up (if possible) and avail the aforementioned to the offending parties? This is what believing, hoping, and enduring looks like as it's not always mental, as in wishing for the best but hoping against hope; even and especially during those times when no hope of rehabilitation seems possible.

In fact, endure means 'to remain, have fortitude, to stay under and/or behind.' Understanding it may not be possible to follow up with everyone you interact with but what about those who are particularly dangerous? Particularly vulnerable? Particularly troublesome? What if you made it a point to remain in that person's life until they became the man or woman of God created them to be?

The Amplified Version says it best when it says, **"Love bears all things [regardless of what comes], believes all things [looking for the best in each one], hopes all things [remaining steadfast during difficult times], endures all things [without weakening]."** Your steadfast hope and efforts may be just what that person needs during their most challenging times. Pray and ask God if this is something He'd like for you to do. In fact, ...

Pray this with me: Heavenly Father, ordinarily I don't get involved in people's lives but if there is ever a time when You need me to connect someone to services, programs, mentors, and/or opportunities INSTEAD of or after making an arrest, please let me know and I'll do whatever I can...with Your help. In Jesus' name.

Love Never Fails

There is never anything that you do, that when done with love, which will not succeed. Ever. That being said, should you choose to police in the God-kind-of-love, you will never fail, fall short, or be unprotected, simply because you are doing it God's way.

The most important thing about love that you need to remember is that God loves you and He always will. Typically, thoughts of His love come while your off duty or while you're with loved ones. But as someone who lives in harm's way, you sir/ma'am, especially need to be reminded of how overly protective God's love really is. Romans 8:35-39 says,

> [35] **Who shall separate [you] from the love of Christ? Shall tribulation, or distress, or persecution, or famine, or nakedness, or peril, or sword?...Yet in all these things [you] are more than [a] conqueror through Him who love[s] [you].**

[38] For [you need to be]... persuaded that neither [fear of] death nor life, nor angels nor [fear of] principalities nor powers, nor things present nor things to come, [39] nor height nor depth, nor any other created thing, shall be able to separate [you] from the love of God which is in Christ Jesus [your] Lord [whether on duty or off].

And remember: "**...God has not given [you] a spirit of fear...**' So don't be afraid to become an officer of love instead of just an officer of the law. God has given you the power to police, in love with a sound mind. And with that sound mind, let's continue our study of 2 Timothy 1:7 and dive into sound mindedness.

Sound Mindedness

A simple definition of a **sound mind** is to have peace of mind. Colossians 3:15 in the Amplified Version says,

> 'And let the peace (soul harmony which comes) from Christ rule (act as umpire continually) in your heart [deciding and settling with finality all questions that arise in your mind, in that peaceful state] to which as [members of Christ's] one body you were also called [to live]. And be thankful (appreciative), [giving praise to God always].'

According to the Fellowship of Christian Peace Officers' website, there are approximately 86,000 law enforcement officers [11] who profess to be Christians. Therefore, as a member of this subset of officers you should wholeheartedly believe in Colossians 3:12 which says, '**...as the elect of God, [chosen to work in law enforcement you should] ...put on tender mercies, kindness, humility, meekness, longsuffering... [and love].**' The fact that you are a Peace Officer, coupled with the fact that Jesus, who is the Prince of Peace, is Your Lord and Savior, you're going to have to practice letting, '**...the peace (soul harmony which comes) from Christ rule (act as umpire continually) in your heart [while on duty and allowing that peace to decide and settle with finality all questions [about any subject, suspect, surrounding, environment, and/or situation] that [may] arise in your mind, in that peaceful state]**. Notice it says, '**in that peaceful state**' and not from a state of fear. Therefore, during those moments when you have to make split-second decisions, you can do so from a place of peace.

What if those 516,000 officers, who inflicted serious bodily injury and/or death on those they swore to protect and to serve, had chosen instead to make those split-second decisions from a place of peace? What if during those moments he or she remembered God's power to protect both of them, and the public, and instead chose to de-escalate the situation instead of acting out of fear? What if, for a moment, those officers remembered that God not only loves them (the officer) but those in which they injured and/or killed? Understanding that in those moments *all* of the aforementioned may not be possible but ***one*** should at least come to mind. And if one doesn't, then that should be a tale tell sign that the officer needs to spend more time in prayer and in God's Word. And please know, this is in no way an attempt to bash and/or condemn law enforcement. But some attention needs to be brought to the fact that both they, and/or YOU, are still badge carrying children of our Heavenly Father. That being said…

Your confession and your profession are inseparable.

You should never set aside your confession of faith while wearing your uniform. In fact, you should remind yourself daily – as you put on your uniform and badge – that you are a fearless child of the Most High God and that you will enforce the law by grace, in faith.

Because when we, the public, hear that you were afraid, we lose hope. Only because when we think of the 18,000 law enforcement agencies, we tend to believe that all 860,000 sworn police personnel are fearless. In the minds of most, fearlessness is a prerequisite of the job. In our minds, every agent has had fearlessness training and/or has passed fear-filled tests. We assume that because you wear that badge, that you somehow are endowed with courage. We assume that because many times you come to our rescue when we're afraid. So, to discover that many of your decisions were rooted in fear is disheartening. But can I tell you something? God never intended for you to enforce the law frightened. He never intended for you to have to do your job afraid because as mentioned earlier, when you do, you're seeing the situation, and us, through a cloudy lens and as such, will be prone to make fear-based decisions based on a falsehood. Thus, the old adage, "fear clouds judgment" holds true.

An example of how fear clouds judgment can be found in Matthew 14:25-33 which reads,

> ²⁵ Now in the fourth watch of the night Jesus went to them, walking on the sea. ²⁶ And when the disciples saw Him walking on the sea, they were troubled, saying, "It is a ghost!" And they cried out for fear. ²⁷ But immediately Jesus spoke to them, saying, "Be of good cheer! It is I; do not be afraid."
>
> ²⁸ And Peter answered Him and said, "Lord, if it is You, command me to come to You on the water." ²⁹ So He said, "Come." And when Peter had come down out of the boat, he walked on the water to go to Jesus. ³⁰ But when he saw that the wind was boisterous, he was afraid; and beginning to sink he cried out, saying, "Lord, save me!" ³¹ And immediately Jesus stretched out His hand and caught him, and said to him, "O you of little faith, why did you doubt?" ³² And when they got into the boat, the wind ceased.
>
> ³³ Then those who were in the boat came and worshiped Him, saying, "Truly You are the Son of God."

Here we have Jesus doing something that was molecularly impossible. The Lord was walking on water. And not just any water; He was walking on water in the midst of hurricane-like conditions. Not that it mattered but in the words of Justice Rehnquist, this was definitely a "tense, uncertain and rapidly evolving situation." Yet the Lord stood firm while Peter sank. Though confident he could do what he was seeing the Lord do, '...**when he saw that the wind was boisterous, he [became] afraid.**' Hence, the result of looking at the situation through the eyes of fear and not faith. Had he kept his eyes on Jesus, he would have continued to walk by faith. Yet fear caused him to not only doubt himself, but the Lord.

Your Spiritual Body Armor

In order to do your job effectively and fearlessly, you are going to have to police by faith. Meaning, you're not moved by "tense, uncertain and rapidly evolving situations." **'For we walk by faith, [and] not by sight.'** (2 Cor. 5:7) Again, that just doesn't apply to when your off duty but especially while you're on. You can walk into high intensity situations knowing that you're fully protected - spirit, soul, and body. But how can you be so sure? Ephesians 6:11-18 answers that for us. It reads,

> 'Put on the whole armor of God, that you may be able to stand against the wiles of the devil. [12] For [you're] not wrestling against flesh and blood, but against principalities, against powers, against the rulers of the darkness of this age, against spiritual hosts of wickedness in the heavenly places. [13] Therefore take up the whole armor of God, that you may be able to withstand [while on the job] ...and having done all, to stand.
>
> [14] Stand therefore, having girded your waist with truth, having put on the breastplate of righteousness, [15] and having shod your feet with the preparation of the gospel of peace; [16] above all, taking the shield of faith with which you will be able to quench all the fiery darts of the wicked one. [17] And take the helmet of salvation, and the sword of the Spirit, which is the word of God; [18] praying always with all prayer and supplication in the Spirit, being watchful to this end with all perseverance and supplication for all the saints—"

One way to ensure you're protected each day is to put on the whole armor of God. Each day, before you put on your uniform, you should first...

> 'Put on the whole armor of God, that you may be able to stand against the wiles of the devil.

The armor in question can be likened to body armor only this armor is spiritual because again, the fear in which you're battling is spiritual as well. Since we've already established that whenever you sense fear, you are sensing a spirit, it only makes sense to have something to counter that spirit which is faith in the whole armor of God.

> [12] For [you're] not wrestling against flesh and blood, but against principalities, against powers, against the rulers of the darkness of this age, against spiritual hosts of wickedness in the heavenly places.

So that you can better understand that verse, it could now read:

> **You're not only wrestling against subjects and suspects, but against spiritual principalities...powers...rulers of the darkness...[and] spiritual hosts of wickedness that are controlling and/or influencing their behavior.**

As mentioned before, behavior can be influenced by spirits of whom are governed by **principalities...powers...rulers of the darkness of this age [and]...spiritual hosts of wickedness in the heavenly places.**

Waist Armor

[13] Therefore [you need to] take up the whole armor of God, that you may be able to withstand [while on the job] and having done all, to stand...having girded your waist with truth.

Notice the first piece of the armor that's described is the waist. Had the officers who took it upon themselves to have sex with detainees put on this part of their spiritual body armor everyday, there perhaps would be no need for the *Closing the Law Enforcement Consent Loophole Act* of 2022.

Previously we discussed a weightlifting belt which is worn as, '**a reminder to keep your spine in the correct position and can help maintain abdominal pressure to stabilize the spine during heavy lifting.**' [12] This is how you should see your waist. That spiritual belt of truth is there to remind you to keep your spirit and demeanor in the correct posture so that you can maintain control over your emotions while you're under pressure and during those complex situations when split-second decisions are needed. And though being truthful can often seem heavy, Jesus said, "Come to Me, all you who labor and are heavy laden, and I will give you rest. [29] Take My yoke upon you and learn from Me, for I am gentle and lowly in heart, and you will find rest for your souls. [30] For My yoke is easy and My burden is light." (Mt. 11:28-30) If you'd just ask, the Lord will help take the dark complexity out of policing as well as teach you how to police in truth. So...

Pray this with me: Heavenly Father, I've been told, and even believe, that policing is a heavy, complex and tiresome job but Your Word says that if I come to You, that You would give me rest. So Lord, I ask You to teach me how to rest in You while I serve and protect. You said to take Your yoke, so I ask that You remove the one I've worn for so long and that You would teach me how to be gentle and lowly in the position I am in. Lord, You said that Your yoke is easy, and Your burden is light, so I ask that You remove the burdensomeness of the job and that You make policing easy for me, my partner, and for Your children within the department. I thank You for it. In Jesus' name.

I know it sounds strange to pray and ask God to take a difficult and dangerous job and make it into something seemingly impossible. But it's not so much that God will make policing easy, but He will equip and anoint you with light on how to do it more effectively. He won't turn it into a game but there will be an ease with which you go about your duties. But that can only come by LEARNING FROM Him. In order for Him to do that, you're going to have to spend some time with Him – in prayer and in study. The more you do, the more He'll teach you about Him, about you in Him, and Him protecting you as you protect others.

Bulletproof Breastplate of Righteousness

The next piece of the spiritual body armor that should be worn is, '**...the breastplate of righteousness.**' The righteousness in which you do your job should not be self-righteous, in the sense that because you are in law enforcement, you believe that you are better, more righteous, more law-abiding, or morally inept than those in whom you serve. Your righteousness should not be determined by your badge but in Christ Jesus who made you righteous.

> '**...we are ambassadors for Christ, as though God were pleading through us: we implore you on Christ's behalf, be reconciled to God. [21] For He made Him who knew no sin to be sin for us, that we might become the righteousness of God in Him.**' - 2 Cor. 5:20, 21

Peacekeeping Foot Gear

The third piece of armor has to do with the way you patrol as it speaks of your foot gear. Verse 15 states, '**...having shod your feet with the preparation of the gospel of peace.**' This lets us know that when you enter into every situation, your first and/or default stance should be that of **peace**. You should go into every interaction with a genuine desire to de-escalate the situation and see if any peaceful alternatives are available. Again, as an officer of the peace, whose Lord and Savior is the Prince of Peace, you should excel when it comes to peaceful resolutions, of which include addressing disparities, promoting safety for underserved communities, distributing equitable justice, being culturally aware and promoting reparative justices for vulnerable populations.

Shield of Faith

> '**...above all, taking the shield of faith with which you will be able to quench all the fiery darts of the wicked one.**'

This piece is probably the most important piece as it speaks to your protection. The shield of faith is analogous to a bullet proof vest. In fact, when this verse was written the Apostle Paul was incarcerated and was writing inside his cell while looking at a Roman guard's shield. During that time, Roman shields were so large that they enclosed a soldier's entire body. Though your tactical gear (i.e., bulletproof vest) serves the same purpose, this shield is able to **quench all the fiery darts** which means though you're protected, this shield serves as a backup to ensure that nothing penetrates, no matter the fire power or location of the bullet. How is this possible? Because this shield relies on your faith.

Matthew 9:27-29 says,

> **[27] When Jesus departed from there, two blind men followed Him, crying out and saying, "Son of David, have mercy on us!" [28] And when He had come into the house, the blind men came to Him. And Jesus said to them,** "Do you believe that I am able to do this?" **They said to Him, "Yes, Lord." [29] Then**

He touched their eyes, saying, "According to your faith let it be to you." **³⁰ And their eyes were opened.**

The two blind men mentioned here received their sight based upon their belief that Jesus was able heal. The same is true for you. ***God's ability to protect you depends upon your faith in His ability to do so.*** Your faith in God should determine how you police, not your fear. Your faith in not only His ability, but in His love for you should provide, **'...the peace (the soul harmony which comes) from Christ ruling and acting as (umpire continually) in your heart [while you're on duty and allowing His peace and the knowledge of Him loving you]...decide and settle with finality all questions [about any subject, suspect, or situation] that [may] arise in your mind.'**

The way that you build your faith in God is to spend time with Him daily – in prayer and in His Word. And you need to be sure to Sabbath. There should be at least one day, and not necessarily Saturday or Sunday, that you do nothing but rest and spend time with Your Father. Again, it doesn't have to be on the days that others Sabbath as it depends upon your schedule. But whatever day it is, spend that day with God; either reading the Word, watching, or listening to faith-based programming, reading faith-building books, or resting and meditating on Him and His Word. Though we'll get into other ways to build your faith later, it is important that you begin to settle it in your heart now that you're going to police by faith and not by fear and that you're going to adjust your lifestyle accordingly so that you can grow your faith by spending time with God.

Helmet of Salvation

The next piece of spiritual armor is **'...the helmet of salvation...'** The helmet covers your head in which encapsulates your brain and is the home of your mind. Therefore, this piece of spiritual armor is connected to the mind of your spirit which is also connected to your thought life and the way you think, particularly about your safety and God's ability to protect you.

Salvation in Greek means, 'to be rescued, to be safe, be delivered, or have a defender.' Therefore, what you think about God's ability and desire to protect, rescue, ensure your safety, deliver, and defend you, if need be, needs to be in the forefront of your thoughts daily. The way to ensure that it stays there is to confess these verses before your shift and preferably as you put on your uniform. Be sure to check out the Policing Confessions in the appendix.

Service Weapon of the Spirit

The final piece of armor is, '**...the sword of the Spirit, which is the Word of God.**' The sword of the Spirit is similar to your service weapon, only far more powerful. The same way you rely on and are assured of its ability to protect you is the same assurance you should have in the Word of God.

> '**For the word of God is living and powerful, and sharper than any two-edged sword, piercing even to the division of soul and spirit, and of joints and marrow, and is a discerner of the thoughts and intents of the heart.**' – Hebrews 4:12

God's Word is living which means His Word has life which is important in life-or-death situations. Psalm 118:17 says, **"I shall not die, but live, and declare the works of the Lord."** It's verses like these that you need to remember when you arrive on the scene of an accident or shooting. God's Word just doesn't work for you, but it also works for the community in which you serve.

Notice also that God's Word is powerful. Hebrews 1:1-3 says,

> **God, who at various times and in various ways spoke in time past to the fathers by the prophets, ²has in these last days spoken to us by His Son, whom He has appointed heir of all things, through whom also He made the worlds; ³who being the brightness of His glory and the express image of His person, and <u>upholding all things by the word of His power</u>, when He had by Himself purged our sins, sat down at the right hand of the Majesty on high...**

All things are upheld by the Word of God's power which means the Word of His power is able to keep you out of harm's way. But in order for it to do so, you will need to confess it over your life. Of which, Policing Confessions have been provided for you in the Appendix. #thankmelater

Going back to Hebrews 4:12, God's Word is, '**…sharper than any two-edged sword, piercing even to the division of soul and spirit, and of joints and marrow, and is a discerner of the thoughts and intents of the heart.**' God's Word has the ability to outperform any criminal, weapon, sharp-shooter, and/or sniper on the planet. Not only that but His Word has the ability to '**discern…the thoughts and intents of the heart.**' Meaning, during interrogations or on a stop, when you are filled with His Word, it can decipher every code and discern every untruth, every time.

Though you have on the whole armor of God, you'll also need to be careful to, '**…pray…always with all prayer and supplication in the Spirit, being watchful to this end with all perseverance and supplication for all the saints.**' That means you're also responsible for praying for everyone in your department and within your community. So…

Pray this with me: Heavenly Father, I lift up my department and more importantly the community. I now understand that I am not only there to enforce the law but to serve my community. Lord, please teach me how to pray daily for the residents and business owners and show me how to enforce according to what You give me in prayer. In Jesus' name.

SOURCES

1 - "Behavior." *Merriam-Webster Dictionary*, Ninth New Collegiate Merriam-Webster. 1984.

2 - "Unbecoming." *Merriam-Webster Dictionary*, Ninth New Collegiate Merriam-Webster. 1984.

3, 12 – "Healthy Lifestyle - Healthy Lifestyle." *Mayo Clinic*, Mayo Foundation for Medical Education and Research.

4 - "Provoke." *Merriam-Webster Dictionary*, Ninth New Collegiate Merriam-Webster. 1984.

5 - Dallas Population and Demographic Stats - "Dallas, TX." *Data USA*.

6-"Religious Landscape Study." *Pew Research Center's Religion & Public Life Project*, Pew Research Center, 13 June 2022.

"2019 Poverty Guidelines." *ASPE*.

7, 9-Wikipedia contributors. "Demographics of Dallas–Fort Worth." Wikipedia, The Free Encyclopedia. Wikipedia, The Free Encyclopedia, 14 Sep. 2022. Web. 19 Nov. 2022.

8- McCann, Adam. "2022's Best & Worst Cities for People with Disabilities." *WalletHub*, 27 Sept. 2022.

10-"Watch Nightline Season 40 Episode 249 Thursday, Dec 19, 2019 Online." *ABC*.

11- "We Believe Less than 10% of Cops Nationwide Are Christians." *Fellowship of Christian Peace Officers*.

Chapter 10: Use-of-Force Incidences in the Bible

So far, we've covered:

- The Code of Silence
- Officer Suicides
- Objective Reasoning, Lawful Orders, Probable Cause & Use of Force
- Tennessee v. Garner and Graham v. Connor
- The Objective Reasonableness Behind the Use of Fearful Force
- Fear in Policing, and...
- Policing in Love

Now let's take a quick look at a few use-of-force incidents in the Word.

Empty Hand Control, Soft Use-of-Force Technique

In Acts 23, we find an empty-hand control, soft use-of-force technique being used on the Apostle Paul. It reads,

> '...Paul, looking earnestly at the council, said, "Men and brethren, I have lived in all good conscience before God until this day." ² And the high priest Ananias commanded those who stood by him to strike him on the mouth. ³ Then Paul said to him, "God will strike you, you whitewashed wall! For you sit to judge me according to the law, and do you command me to be struck contrary to the law?"
>
> ⁴ And those who stood by said, "Do you revile God's high priest?" ⁵ Then Paul said, "I did not know, brethren, that he was the high priest; for it is written, 'You shall not speak evil of a ruler of your people.' " ⁶ But when Paul perceived that one part were Sadducees and the other Pharisees, he cried out in the council, "Men and brethren, I am a Pharisee, the son of a Pharisee; concerning the hope and resurrection of the dead I am being judged!"
>
> ⁷ And when he had said this, a dissension arose between the Pharisees and the Sadducees; and the assembly was divided...when there arose a great dissension, the

commander, fearing lest Paul might be pulled to pieces by them, commanded the soldiers to go down and take him by force...and bring him into the barracks.'

Here we find Paul making a court appearance in which he is struck by one of the jurors. After which, he continues to plead his case when the courtroom erupts causing the bailiffs and other sheriff's deputies *"to [have to] take him by force...and bring him into custody.'* The type of force used was an empty-hand control soft technique in which an officer simply 'grabs, holds and/or joint locks' in order *'to gain control of a situation.'* [1] Again, this was a soft technique that was neither excessive nor deadly and thankfully did not result in injury and/or death which means it may not have been reported to the FBI's Uniform Crime Reporting Program.

Use of Force Resulting in Serious Bodily Injury

In John 18 the decision was made to arrest, prosecute, and kill Jesus. The reason: Jewish officials had determined that since the Lord wasn't licensed to minister, He should be prosecuted to the highest extent of the law. And though one might assume Jesus was licensed to preach, He was not. And because He wasn't officially ordained, He was indicted. But why a criminal indictment? Shouldn't the fact that a Jewish citizen exercised His civil right to speak publicly about His faith be a civil matter? Glad you asked and yes, it was. Yet these officials chose to charge Jesus *criminally* over what should have been a *civil* matter. So, they brought four charges against the Lord. They charged Him with **(1) Criminal Impersonation, (2) Felony Tax Evasion, (3) Destruction of Property,** and **(4) Blasphemy**. The felony charges, Criminal Impersonation and Felony Tax Evasion, would have carried 9 years of federal time while the misdemeanor charges of Destruction of Property and Blasphemy, carried a maximum of 11 years. Thus, at max, Jesus should have served 20 years. Yet, they sought the death penalty. But why is this important? Because it sheds light on how – still to this day - laws are used to wrongfully sentence and harshly over sentence for what could possibly be civil matters.

When an officer puts someone in a chokehold for selling cigarettes outside of a convenience store, that could have been a civil matter. When an officer uses deadly force for violation of a city ordinance simply because someone is selling CD's outside of a liquor store, that too is a civil matter. Yet both Eric Garner and Alton Sterling lost their lives.

While in custody for what should have been a civil matter, Jesus was transported to the home of '**Annas...the father-in-law of Caiaphas**,' the high priest. After several unsuccessful attempts to locate witnesses to corroborate their false allegations, the high priest decided to personally interrogate the Lord. During his interrogation he, '**...asked Jesus about His [staff] and His [teachings]. Jesus [then] answered him, "I [taught publicly]** ...and in secret I...said nothing. Why do you ask Me? Ask those who...heard Me...they know what I said."** When He said that, '**...one of the officers...struck Jesus...**' Thus, Jesus was physically assaulted by an officer while in police custody. Shortly thereafter He was wrongly convicted and sentenced to death; only to be assaulted again by a gang of officers in Mark 14:64 and 65.

> '**...[and] they all condemned Him to be deserving of death. ⁶⁵ Then some began to spit on Him, and to blindfold Him, and to beat Him, and to say to Him, "Prophesy!" And the officers struck Him with the palms of their hands.**'

Thus, establishing that the Lord was a victim of police violence. Had this been reported to the FBI's Uniform Crime Reporting Program, it would have been identified as a serious bodily injury use-of-force incident resulting from warrant services or a court order.

In Acts 16:16-23 we find another use-of-force incident as it reads,

> '**¹⁶ Now it happened, as we went to prayer, that a certain slave girl possessed with a spirit of divination met us, who brought her masters much profit by fortune-telling. ¹⁷ This girl followed...us...saying, "These men are the servants of the Most High God, who proclaim to us the way of salvation." ¹⁸ And this she did for many days. But Paul, greatly annoyed, turned and said to the spirit, "I command you in the name of Jesus Christ to come out of her." And he [the spirit of divination] came out that very hour. ¹⁹ But when her masters saw that their hope of profit was gone, they seized Paul and Silas and dragged them into the marketplace to the authorities. ²⁰ And they brought them to the magistrates, and**

said, "These men, being Jews, exceedingly trouble our city; ²¹ and they teach customs which are not lawful for us, being Romans, to receive or observe." ²² Then the...magistrates... commanded them to be beaten with rods. ²³ And when they had laid many stripes on them, they threw them into prison, commanding the jailer to keep them securely.'

Here we have Paul and Silas, two ministers of the gospel, hosting a conference when they encounter a teenage influencer. Though she was giving their event free advertisement to her millions of followers, her public proclamations led to a lot of negative publicity. So much so, local business owners accused Paul and Silas of wrongdoing and demanded their arrest, to which law enforcement obliged. When taken into custody both men were brutally beaten, but why? At the request of prominent business owners because according to them, **"These men, being Jews, exceedingly trouble [the] city..."** So, was it what they were preaching or was it the fact that Paul and Silas were Jews? The answer to that question is both. Therefore, Paul and Silas were victims of police brutality because they were racially profiled. And thus, we see another example of use-of-force resulting in serious bodily injury which by the way would have been included in the Uniform Crime Reporting Program as the officer was responding to unlawful or suspicious activities.

Use of Deadly Force

An example of deadly force can be found in Mark 6 which tells of the account of John the Baptist and King Herod. John, a leading minister, disapproved of Herod's marriage to his deceased brother's wife, to which Herod decided to lock John up. While incarcerated, Herod's stepdaughter/niece danced for her stepfather and his adult friends. Such dancing would be similar to a strip tease today. Because her dancing pleased her uncle/stepfather, he told her that he would give her anything she wanted - even '...**up to half [of his] kingdom**.' Because she was underage, she inquired of her mother what she should ask for. Her mother advised her to ask that John be killed. The girl takes her mother's advice, to which Herod commands he be, '...**beheaded...in prison**.'

Ordinarily, when we read that account, we only focus on the fact that John was killed for no real reason. We often miss the fact that this happened while he was incarcerated, at the hands of law enforcement. Yet another example of use-of-force – deadly force, resulting from a court order.

As you can see, police brutality and use-of-force incidences did occur in the Bible. As such, as someone in law enforcement, you can be assured that there is Bible instruction on how to enforce the law – as both a child of God and as someone who follows Christ. Let's now take a look at examples of good officers throughout scripture.

SOURCES

1-"The Use-of-Force Continuum." *National Institute of Justice.*

Chapter 11: Good Cops

In the same way we took the time to review officer misconduct byway of wrongful use-of-force, I think it's only fair that we review officers of love. Go with me to Acts 10, where we find an example of a Bible-believing, faith-filled lieutenant by the name of Cornelius.

> **There was a certain man in Caesarea called Cornelius, a centurion of what was called the Italian Regiment, [2] a devout man and one who feared God with all his household, who gave alms generously to the people, and prayed to God always. [3] About the ninth hour of the day he saw clearly in a vision an angel of God coming in and saying to him, "Cornelius!"**
>
> **[4] And when he observed him, he was afraid, and said, "What is it, lord?" So he said to him, "Your prayers and your alms have come up for a memorial before God. [5] Now send men to Joppa, and send for Simon whose surname is Peter. [6] He is lodging with Simon, a tanner, whose house is by the sea. He will tell you what you must do." [7] And when the angel who spoke to him had departed, Cornelius called two of his household servants and a devout soldier from among those who waited on him continually. [8] So when he had explained all these things to them, he sent them to Joppa.**

Here we have Cornelius, '...**a centurion of...the Italian Regiment, a devout man and one who feared God with all his household, who gave alms generously to the people, and prayed to God always**.' The first thing we need to know about Cornelius is that he is nothing like the centurion we learned about in chapter 1. Cornelious is a **devout man**. **Devout** in Greek means, 'dutiful or pious.' Typically, when you think of someone being devout, you tend to only think in terms of religious piety, but it also has to do with work ethic. Hence, the term 'dutiful.' Dutiful means to be 'motivated by a sense of duty.' His duty as a centurion was to command one hundred men which consisted of 80 legionaries and 20 servants. 'Roman legionaries were viewed as the foremost fighting force in the Roman world' [1] which means he was responsible for leading, training, commanding, and disciplining one hundred of some of the world's finest fighters. This also was a man who was highly respected, without corruption; one who had infallible integrity.

Secondly, Cornelius was also known as a man who, **'feared God.'** But this isn't fear in the sense of being frightened or afraid. Fear, as it's used here, means respect, reverence, and honor. Perhaps this is a good time to recommend that you read John Bevere's 'Awe of God', but I digress. Ordinarily, that wouldn't be that much of a big deal but because there were an 'array of gods…spirits…and foreign cults' [2] being practiced in Rome, this is very significant because at the time, the Israelites were under Roman occupation. Therefore, for a Roman centurion to fear the God of a people whose nation had been taken captive, was unheard of. That would be the same as a Russian general, during the Russo-Ukrainian war, whose troops were now occupying the Donbas Luhansk regions of Ukraine who not only gave generously to the Ukrainian people, but also prayed to the God of the Ukrainian Jews as well as believed in His Son Jesus. Yes, that's how the headlines would read today. Therefore, this verse could now read,

> **'a Roman military general, known for his outstanding work ethic, who's people were known for mythology and cultish practices, reverenced, honored, and served the God of Abraham, Isaac, and Jacob.'**

That gives you a clearer understanding of who Cornelius was and why his story is significant.

The third thing we know about this officer is that he **'gave alms generously to the people'** which means he financially supported nonprofits, places of worship, the homeless, and other vulnerable communities. Think about that for a moment. A high-ranking officer known for protecting and SERVING the community. But not just giving back, he's known for his generosity. He saw a need in his community and did something about it. He recognized how important places of worship were to the Jews, so he built a synagogue. This high-ranking officer personally financed a multimillion-dollar church, of sorts today.

As a citizen, we tend to think of law enforcement in either one of two ways: very ethical or ineptly corrupt.

But no one builds a church for no reason. Yes, there could have been tax incentives, but this man genuinely believed in what and Who was needed. He wasn't doing this for fame, notoriety, publicity, or for the likes. He was truly a man of God. And let's not overlook his work ethic, which is something I think we take for granted in policing today.

Coupled with his outstanding work ethic, we can readily see, he was nothing like the officers we hear about today.

Work ethic not only applies to morality but doing the work ethically.

Ethically in the sense that abiding by the Word of God is more important than adhering to the code of silence. Ethically in the sense that you protect and SERVE all people as opposed to those who hold your same political views, ideology, or skin color.

I encourage you to reread the chapter on *Objective Reasoning* again in light of what you just discovered but let's get back to our discussion on Cornelius who the Bible refers to as...

> '...a centurion of...the Italian Regiment, a devout man and one who feared God with all his household, who gave alms generously to the people, and prayed to God always.'

Again, we're discussing Cornelius and good policing. Notice the scripture says that Cornelius, **'prayed to God always.'** Don't take that lightly. Here's an officer that prays but notice how he prays...**always.** Which means even whether he was on the job, drafting a report, or in the community, he was always seeking the Lord for answers and direction which lets us know that his decisions were made with the help of the Holy Spirit.

Cornelius' Leadership Style and Staff

When you read the rest of Acts 10, you'll also discover that not only did he pray, but he fasted too.

³⁰ So Cornelius said, "Four days ago I was fasting until this hour; and at the ninth hour I prayed in my house, and behold, a man stood before me in bright clothing, ³¹ and said, 'Cornelius, your prayer has been heard, and your alms are remembered in the sight of God.' - v. 30, 31

And this is a great point. *To be a high-ranking law enforcement official requires prayer and fasting.* That's because when it comes to positions of leadership, you need that type of consecration and closeness with God so that you can hear how to respond in life-or-death situations. You also need the wisdom of God to know how to lead and how to interact with the various cultures and those who don't worship, think or act like you. Cornelius' approach to leadership was not a one-size-fits-all. He sought God.

Because he followed God, it showed up in his ability to influence his staff. In Acts 10:7,8 we get a bird's eye view into the lives of those he led when it read, **'And when the angel who spoke to him had departed, Cornelius called two of his household servants and a devout soldier from among those who waited on him continually. So when he had explained all these things to them, he sent them to Joppa.'** Notice that a member of his staff was described as **devout**. Devout again means, *'dutiful or pious'* which lets us know that he too was faithful and operated in integrity; much like his Chief. He too feared and prayed to God.

This man worked alongside Cornelius both professionally and privately which meant he knew the ins and outs of both his personal and private affairs. Yet the Bible refers to them both as devout which lets us know whether on and off the job, these officers were men of God. These verses also let us know that it is possible for law enforcement personnel to live in accordance with God's standards. And just so you know, it is our responsibility - as citizens of the community - to pray for and over our local police department, who have sworn to protect and serve us. Even though there may some rotten apples who may not be walking in biblical integrity today, these verses give us hope and biblical precedence that it is possible.

If you're in leadership or law enforcement…

Pray this with me: Heavenly Father, I desire to lead, protect and to serve like Cornelius. Show me ways that I can be more devout, reverent, and serve You. Show me what's needed in the community and with citizens as a whole. Lead me to places where I can give, and more importantly Lord, teach me how to pray. I've heard that prayer is just talking to You, so Lord, I'm going to start talking to You more, on the job. In Jesus' name.

Good job! Now I challenge you to look for opportunities to serve the community in which you've been charged to protect. Ask God to show you ways you can be known as a servant officer and a generous giver; whether it's giving of your time, talent, or money. To make sure that you do...

Pray this with me: Heavenly Father, show me how to become a generous giver. Lord, I'm willing to give my time, of my talent, and even my money, if need be. Because I want to not only protect my community but serve as well. In Jesus' name.

For citizens reading this...

Pray this with me: Heavenly Father, I see that both Cornelius and this other officer were faithful men of God which lets me know that it possible to have officers and high-ranking officials with the same character traits within my community. Lord, though they may not be living according to Your standard now, I pray that You would send Peter's into their lives so that they too can be saved, filled with Your Holy Spirit, and live as devout examples within our community. In Jesus' name.

Let's take a look at another good cop in Matthew 8:5-13. Here we find a lieutenant and quite possibly a captain, interacting with Jesus. When you examine the text, you'll discover the interesting posture of the high-ranking official. It reads,

> 'Now when Jesus had entered Capernaum, a centurion came to Him, pleading with Him, ⁶ saying, "Lord, my servant is lying at home paralyzed, dreadfully tormented." ⁷ And Jesus said to him, "I will come and heal him." ⁸ The centurion answered and said, "Lord, I am not worthy that You should come under my roof. But only speak a word, and my servant will be healed.... ¹⁰ When Jesus heard it, He marveled, and said to those who followed, "Assuredly, I say to you, I have not found such great faith, not even in Israel!"

Notice verse 6 says, "**Lord, my servant is lying at home paralyzed, dreadfully tormented.**" When you dissect their interaction, you can readily see the officer's posture of humility when he first approaches Jesus as he refers to Him as **Lord**. Because he was a high-ranking, well-respected law enforcement official, he could have easily addressed Jesus by name and said, "Jesus, one of my officers is at home sick." Yet he addresses Him as Lord - a sign of immediate respect.

After paying homage, he then shows compassion for his direct report by explaining his condition. Jesus then agrees to make a house visit, but the centurion takes his humility a step further by saying, **"Lord, I am not worthy that You should come under my roof."** Again, referencing Jesus as Lord and explaining why he doesn't believe he's worthy enough to be under the same roof as Jesus. Think about that for a moment. A high-ranking official so meek that he doesn't deem himself worthy to be in close proximity to the Lord. Today, many officers enter homes without search warrants, will stop-and-frisk, or take other liberties, at will. Yet this officer doesn't abuse his power, which lets us know that it is possible to believe the same for our local police departments today.

Another point is that he could have also **commanded** Jesus to come and heal his direct report. Remember the Jews had been captured and taken as political prisoners. Back then, a Roman officer could command a citizen to carry a particular item or run an errand of a mile or less. This was required of both Roman and Jewish citizens which is why Jesus said, "…whoever compels you to go one mile, go with him two." (Mt. 5:41) Instead of compelling the Lord, he simply releases his faith by saying, **"Lord… only speak a word, and my servant will be healed."** And though we can get into the great faith this officer exhibited, the one thing we need to walk away with is that it's possible for law enforcement to demonstrate meekness in the presence of others.

Never should an officer think him/herself to be higher than any other citizen, regardless as to your state invested power. Officers should be required to refer to every citizen by name and never call them racial slurs or make them feel less than. Yet many times this is the case, and such is the time. But if we, as believers, come together and begin to confess and believe that God can change their hearts and minds, then officers within our respective communities will become more like this centurion and respect us as human beings.

Pray this with me: Heavenly Father, I lift up every officer within our community and state and ask that You'd please forgive them of their pride. I ask that You'd teach them spiritual servanthood so that it will correlate into their public service. In Jesus' name.

There is yet another example of good policing which can be found in Acts 27. Here we witness Paul's extradition. Notice verses 42 and 43 says, '**And the soldiers' plan was to kill the prisoners, lest any of them should swim away and escape. ⁴³ But the centurion, wanting to save Paul, kept them from their purpose.**' This group of officers were planning on killing the prisoners because in Roman times, a soldier would be put to death if a prisoner escaped. Therefore, in order to save their careers, they were willing to kill them. Yet their lieutenant, '…**kept them from their purpose.**' Even though it would have been easier to just kill them, this lieutenant/centurion did the right thing which means it's possible for officers to not shoot fleeing suspects because again, we live in an advanced society where tools are readily available to locate the suspect at a later date.

"

> You may have heard that some people down in the prep school wrote some racial slurs on the message boards. If you're outraged by those words, then you're in the right place. That kind of behavior has no place at prep school. It has no place in the United State Air Force. You should be outraged not only as an airman but as a human being. And we would all be naïve to think that everything is perfect here. We would be naïve to think that we shouldn't discuss this topic. We would also be tone deaf not to think about the backdrop of what's going on in our country. Things like Charlottesville and Ferguson, the protests in the NFL. So just in case you're unclear on where I stand on this topic, I'm going to leave you with my most important thought today.

If you can't treat someone with dignity and respect, then you need to get out. If you can't treat someone from another gender, whether that's man or a woman, with dignity and respect, then you need to get out. If you demean someone in any way, then you need to get out. And if you can't treat someone from another race or a different color skin with dignity and respect, then you need to get out. Reach for your phones...because I want you to use it so that we can all have the MORAL COURAGE together...what we should have is a civil discourse and talk about these issues...we have a better idea and it's about diversity. The power of us as a diverse group...the power that we come from all walks of life, from all parts of the country, that we come from all races, we come from all backgrounds, gender, all makeup, all upbringing, the power of that diversity comes together and makes us that more powerful.

- Retired Lieutenant General Jay B. Silveria
Speech given to Air Force Academy in 2017

"

SOURCES

1-Wikipedia contributors. "Legionary." *Wikipedia, The Free Encyclopedia.* Wikipedia, The Free Encyclopedia, 14 July. 2021. Web. 4 Dec. 2022.

2-Wasson, Donald L. "Roman Religion." *Ancient History Encyclopedia*, Ancient History Encyclopedia, 2 Dec. 2022.

Chapter 12: Psychological Evaluations

There's something to be said about the mindset of an officer, whether good or bad. As mentioned in *'What's Love Got To Do With...Law Enforcement,'* the ideology of use-of-force begins during the recruiting process. When an applicant is asked – during an interview - if they're willing to kill someone, this sets the expectation that deadly force may be used in the future. Notwithstanding that the likelihood of force being used is high, we shouldn't take for granted that all applicants and/or recruits are psychologically capable of making that decision.

Again, in the City of Dallas, after an applicant has successfully completed a;

- Civil Service Written Test
- Preliminary Interview Questionnaire
- Physical Fitness Test
- Pre-Polygraph Questionnaire
- Passed the Polygraph Exam
- Gone before the Interview Review Board, and...
- Passed the Background Check

They are then extended a conditional offer letter contingent upon successful completion of the next phase which curtails passing a:

- Psychological Exam
- Medical Exam, and...
- Drug Screen [1]

As a civilian, this process seems arduous. Even so, there's a few dings in the process that should be a cause for concern.

First and foremost, the psychological exam isn't conducted until the department has invested two to four MONTHS of the department's time and resources. This is so that an extensive background investigation can be carried out. At this point, the department is now heavily invested in the applicant which means by this time they may be willing to overlook or make exceptions to the remaining parts of the process (i.e., the psychological exam). But why is this cause for concern?

The Psychology of an Applicant

According to the American Psychological Association, *psychology* is defined as, *'the study of the mind and behavior.'* [2] It is *'the supposed collection of behaviors, traits, attitudes...that characterize an individual.'* [3] Prior to investing months to investigate an applicant's *history*, perhaps it would be best to invest that time assessing how the applicant thinks *today*. Real-world assessments that assess their ideology and temperament particularly when it comes to serving and protecting the people who consists of 2 genders, 7 different races, 23 sexual orientations, 5 political parties, 5 economic/income classes, 4,200 religions, and 8 main types of people with disabilities. Though certain parts of the assessment can be written, much like officers go through real-world simulations in the academy, an applicant should be required to prove their thought processes and responses when faced with real-life situations. If departments would invest into this type of evaluation on the front-end of the applicant process, they could perhaps avoid grievances, disciplinary actions, civil lawsuits and criminal cases resulting in hundreds of millions in addition to nationwide television exposure in the future.

And though applicants today are tested on how well they'd respond under high pressure and life-threatening situations; it is more important to assess *how he or she will respond with power.* When given the authority to wear a badge, drive a supped-up patrol car, brandish a weapon, without impunity, how will they conduct themselves with their newfound authority?

Another thing that should be tested is *an officer's patience.* Oftentimes, when an officer gives a lawful order and the person fails to comply, that officer usually takes immediate action, no matter how petty or trivial the matter may be. Though needed and should occur, there are times when as an officer, you should exhibit patience and take the time to listen and consider all aspects. Notwithstanding the danger of policing, there should still be a level of patience required from all ranks.

The patient in spirit is better than the proud in spirit. - Ecc. 7:8

For what credit is it if, when you are beaten for your faults, you take it patiently? But when you do good and suffer, if you take it patiently, this is commendable before God. – 1 Pet. 2:20

An *officer's honesty* should be tested as well. Integrity plays a significant role in law enforcement. Therefore, an applicant's ability, or lack thereof, to tell the truth throughout the vetting process should be an indicator that though this person may be physically, financially, and historically vetted, their ability, or lack thereof, to tell the truth is of utmost importance. And if they've demonstrated the propensity to lie, deceive or tell a half-truth, then perhaps they shouldn't be permitted to move forward. So how do you vet the truth? The first thing is to have them define truth and define a lie. You must first find out if their understanding of the truth differs from that of the department. If the department does not have a clear definition of truth posted, then it cannot expect applicants nor the staff to walk in integrity as truth then becomes relative. Again, truth must clearly be defined and posted.

Another area to consider is service. Since the motto of most police departments is 'to protect and to serve,' applicants should also be tested on their *ability to serve*. Ask applicants about their pet peeves, what they dislike, and then follow up with "How would you protect and serve those whom you don't like and who display peeve-ish tendencies?" The primary focus of policing has been to enforce the law and to protect, but will applicants be able to serve all of the aforementioned populations to which they are assigned? See the Sweet Solution in Appendix [1.2].

Mental Wellness

And while we're on the subject of psychology, it should go without saying that all officers, whether rookie or veteran, should be required to undergo regular mental wellness checks. This is because the basis of objectivity and reasonableness all deal with the mind. Again "in United States criminal law…an objective standard of reasonableness requires the finder of fact to view the circumstances from the standpoint of a hypothetical reasonable person, absent the unique particular physical and psychological characteristics of," said person. [4] Thus, by definition, objective reasoning is mental and relies solely on officers' ability to think objectively. Thus, an officer's mental health must be evaluated regularly to ensure he or she is still capable of reasonableness. With all due respect, it's not fair to assume that once an officer is hired that their mental competence should never be called into question; especially, since as humans, we have the capacity to evolve or devolve, over time. Over time our views change. We can also develop professionally, physically, spiritually, and yes, politically; all of which should be regularly evaluated to ensure an officer is still reasonably able to make sound enforcement decisions. Since so much of their duty involves objectivity, reasonableness, and split-second judgment, all officers should be required to undergo regular mental wellness checks, if for no other reason than to ensure the weight of the job hasn't paid a psychological toll.

SOURCES

1-"Our Excellence Begins with You.'" *Join DPD*.

2, 3 - "APA Dictionary of Psychology." *American Psychological Association*, American Psychological Association.

4 - Wikipedia contributors. "Subjective and objective standard of reasonableness." *Wikipedia, The Free Encyclopedia*. Wikipedia, The Free Encyclopedia, 6 Oct. 2021. Web. 5 Mar. 2022.

Chapter 13: The Defund the Police Movement

We mentioned earlier that in any given situation, a reasonable person will respond in accordance with what's been legally established as acceptable or unacceptable behavior. But even that statement is a point of contention today.

At the time of this writing, there is a nationwide push to, *'Defund the Police.'* Though some would argue it's a socialist attempt to get rid of all police departments, it's actually an effort to reallocate PORTIONS of the present $145.6 billion dollar policing budget into the community, into mental health resources, and into creating affordable housing for the overpoliced.

Yet as a LEO, your sole responsibility deals with the behavior and mental health of those within the community who feel overpoliced. You were trained to enforce the law and in certain cases, correct behavior, and therein lies the problem. You are not a behavioral health expert. Behavioral Health professionals help diagnose and treat people with mental health issues and/or substance use disorders. All of which fall OUTSIDE of your training. Yet so much of what you do hinges upon it. Thus, the goal of the Defund the Police movement was not to leave you jobless, but 'reduce the scope of policing' [1] by relieving you of dealing with 'mental health checks and/or substance-induced disruptive behaviors.' [2]

I mention this because it's possible that up until this point, you only saw yourself as a LEO. But when you get to the heart of what you do, you really enforce the public's adherence to the codified laws that govern behavior. Which inadvertently means that you should either be a qualified behavioral health expert, or your training should be such that you can readily identify when one is needed. An example of this can be found with Damian Daniels.

The Argument for Defund the Police

Damian Daniels was a Black military combat veteran, who in August 2020, was 'shot and killed by a Bexar County Sheriff's Deputy, responding 'to a call for a mental health check.' [3] Mr. Daniels was suicidal and had been 'suffering from PTSD and depression.' [4] Fully aware that he was having a mental health crisis, Mr. Daniels called the Bexar Metropolitan 911 Regional Operations Center and informed them he was having hallucinations. When the sheriff's deputy arrived, Mr. Daniels, stood at his door, with his unconcealed weapon in the holster, saluting the officers who over the next several minutes engage with Mr. Daniels, because they were not clinically trained to deal with his mental state and because they failed to contact a behavioral health professional, the officers decided to take him into custody. Of course, Mr. Daniels resisted because he'd already warned them that he was having hallucinations and it was for this reason that the untrained officers thought it best to taser Mr. Daniels for well over 15-minutes and ultimately shooting him in the chest.

Unfortunately, these officers were not trained in behavioral health. If they were, perhaps they would have realized that Mr. Daniels was not a criminal but a combat veteran having a mental health breakdown. Perhaps, if they were qualified professionals, they would have considered the fact that Mr. Daniels called the police on himself, and instead of a sheriff's department dispatcher dispatching the call to a deputy, perhaps if there was an option to dispatch a trained veteran behavioral health expert, then Mr. Daniels would be alive today. Apart from that, what if the officers had taken his salute as a sign of respect and his stance as a cry for help? Yet because of their own preconceived notions and their lack of objective reasoning, that stance, that respect, and that cry, from a man who fought for our country, went unheeded because instead of being met with compassion or understanding, he was met with force.

A Sweet Solution

If I had my way, there would be legislation passed to protect veterans. Legislation that allows active duty, reserve, and guard forces, along with veterans and retirees to register in a database of sorts. The database would be for the sole purpose of rerouting 911 calls to a behavioral health expert so that instead of a sheriff's deputy arriving on the scene, a trained professional would. And in the event officers encounter someone having a mental health crisis, that person could have a decal of sorts, displayed on their property or vehicle or a card in their wallet, or a dog tag around their neck that could readily identify the type of help they either need and/or quality for. A national database in sync with all municipalities would not only save civilian lives, but the lives of our veterans as well. Imagine if something like that was in place for not only veterans but seniors, known drug users, and the mentally and physically disabled. Instead of officers accessing criminal histories before and/or after arriving at the scene but accessing databases where appropriate personnel can be dispatched and where the public receives the kind of aid they really need. This is what #defundingthepolice looks like in real time. Not taking officer jobs but rerouting services to qualified entities.

It should be noted that the officer who killed Mr. Daniels was acquitted.

SOURCES

1, 2 – "Defund the Police' Made Headlines. What Does It Look like Now?" *CBS News*, CBS Interactive.

3 - *Justice for Darnien Daniols website.*

Chapter 14: Evasions and Escapes

As mentioned before, the City of Dallas is comprised of communities that consist of 28.9% Latino, 28.8% White, 24% African American, '5.9% Asian, 0.6% Native American, 0.1% Pacific Islander, 10.0% from other races, and 2.4% from two or more races.' Forty four percent speak a non-English language, while 80.9% are U.S. citizens. From those communities, 78% profess some sort of Christianity ranging from Protestantism, Catholicism, Mormonism, and Jehovah's Witness; while 4% are either Jewish, Muslim, Buddhist, Hindu or other another religion; with 18% readily identifying themselves as either atheist, agnostic, or nothing in particular. Though the State of Texas fares Republican, as of the November 2022 midterms, Dallas County is primarily Democratic. The median income is $50,627 while the poverty rate stands at 21.8%. That means of its 1.34 million residents, 292,120 live below the national poverty rate of $12,490 for a household of one with Dallas ranking 120 on the best and worst cities in the US for people with disabilities. Notwithstanding, but Dallas is '...also home to the 12th largest lesbian, gay, bisexual and transgender population in the United States.'

With the City of Dallas as our muse, I want you to think of your respective city, in light of your responses from chapter 9. These are vital as your responses are the drivers of how you interact and engage with corresponding communities. To give you an example, if you believe that immigration is a problem and that those who enter the country illegally should be treated in accordance with which they came, then how will you respond when you receive a call involving a Latino? If you believe that African American males are predisposed to commit crimes, then when you interact with a Black man, what are you thinking in the back of your mind? Another paragon is that if you believe that homosexuality is a sin, then how will you engage with those within the LGTBQ community? And if you think that all Muslims are terrorists, how can you provide aid to someone of Arabic descent?

Though these examples seem a bit extreme, believe it or not, if you *have not* done your biblical homework and *have not* made the decision to treat people *as the Word instructs*, you will automatically default to your preconceived notions, which we've already established as the basis of your inability to holistically view people outside of their sex, race, sexual preference, aesthetic, national origin, age, political affiliation, financial status, religion, and/or disability. Hence, to view all people objectively and to set aside what you think they'll probably do (i.e., objective reasoning and probable cause). Again…

The fairest, most objective, and most effective way to view any human being is through the eyes of God.

And as such, should a Latino or African American flee the scene, for whatever reason, you have a decision to make? Will you shoot to kill under the guise of public safety, or will you remember that they too should have a trial before a jury and a chance at life? Will you fire the kill shot or will remember that there are tools available to later locate the suspect? In other words, **will you value their life, or will you take it?**

I make no apology for diving headlong into the chapter topic, but it was important to address this issue head on because this has been the bane of race relations and the approach of so many officers nationwide. There was no time to introduce this chapter much like there was no time given to consider the lives of those fleeing the scene. And this is in no way minimizing the importance of public safety. But let's just see if you have a 360° view of the totality of your decision.

According to the Washington Post, as of November 2022, there were 1,086 police-involved shootings in the US. Sadly, the majority are young, male African Americans between the ages of 20 and 40. [1] Every time I hear of a police-involved shooting, especially when it involves a civilian evading arrest or fleeing the scene, I wonder, why could the officer not let that person get away? It's not as if we're in the 1900's or early 2000's when we didn't have state-of-the-art technology. As mentioned before, we live in a day and age where city surveillance cameras are on every major highway and road. Not only that but we also have real-time location sharing abilities with things like satellite imagery, aerial photography, street maps, 360° interactive panoramic views on every street in addition to real-time views of traffic conditions on every block while simultaneously having the ability to see every route someone could travel by foot, car, bike, air and/or public transportation. [2] Could you not have later reviewed all of the aforementioned to see the route the suspect took? Not only that but there is a Department of Motor Vehicles in every county. Could you not run the plates and visit the address of registration? Why not review those? Yet oftentimes, officers - with high-level security clearances - tend to forget we live in the digital age and instead use deadly force. But again, is deadly force the only option?

When I hear about cases like Daunte Wright, a 20-year-old, who was stopped for a minor traffic violation but was shot by a female officer while trying to flee the scene, I asked myself, why could she not just let him off with a warning or since she'd already ran the plate, why could she not just go to his home after he fled?

When I saw the shooting of Andrew Brown, Jr., a 42-year-old Black man whom 'Pasquotank County Sheriff's Office deputies shot...while serving an arrest warrant,' [3] I thought to myself, *"You were at the man's house. If he fled, let him go. Could you not come back?"* Or most notably George Floyd. A 46-year-old Black man who was 'murdered by former police officer, Derek Chauvin, during an arrest after a store clerk suspected he may have used a counterfeit $20 bill in Minneapolis.'[4] Again, could that officer not have confiscated the fake bill and warned Mr. Floyd never to do it again? Unfortunately, we'll never know the answers to those questions but one question we might be able to answer is: Where does that ideology come from? What is it about an evasion that leads officers to use deadly force?

A Roman Way of Policing

When you think about the fact that police-involved shootings are skyrocketing annually you have to wonder, where does that way of thinking come from? Perhaps Acts 27 can shed some light when it says,

> '**Now when the fourteenth night had come, as we were driven up and down in the Adriatic Sea, about midnight the sailors sensed that they were drawing near some land.... fearing lest we should run aground on the rocks, they dropped four anchors from the stern, and prayed for day to come.** [30] And as the sailors were seeking to escape from the

ship, when they had let down the skiff into the sea, under pretense of putting out anchors from the prow, [31] Paul said to the centurion and the soldiers, "Unless these men stay in the ship, you cannot be saved." [32] Then the soldiers cut away the ropes of the skiff and let it fall off. And the soldiers' plan was to kill the prisoners, lest any of them should swim away and escape. [43] But the centurion, wanting to save Paul, kept them from their purpose...' (v. 27, 30-32, 43)

Notice the soldiers were willing to kill the prisoners when they thought they would escape. Not that they'd overheard a plan but because they anticipated an opportunity, their first thought was to kill the prisoners as opposed to running the risk of escape. But why? As mentioned earlier, according to '...Roman law, a guard who allowed the escape of a prisoner was...put to death' [5] on the basis of dereliction of duty. Thus, the mindset of this guard, as may be the case with officers today, is that to allow any type of evasion would be seen as a dereliction of duty. But the question now becomes where does it specifically state, in an officer's job description, in departmental procedures, or in State or federal statutes, that deadly force can only be used in the event of evasion?

As mentioned in our discussion of *Tennessee v Garner*, the Fourth Amendment says,

> The right of the people to be secure in their persons, houses, papers, and effects, against unreasonable searches and seizures, shall not be violated, and no warrants shall issue, but upon probable cause, supported by oath or affirmation, and particularly describing the place to be searched, and the persons or things to be seized.[6]

Legal scholars, constitutionalists, and lawyers nationwide have taken that to mean that...

> "Under the Fourth Amendment of the U.S. Constitution, a police officer may use deadly force to prevent the escape of a fleeing suspect only if the officer has a good-faith belief that the suspect poses a significant threat of death or serious physical injury to the officer or others." [6]

But again, the problem with the Fourth Amendment is that it only speaks to probable cause which we've already discovered, does not have a federal statutory provision, state statute, or clear definition of the known facts, and/or plausible reasons and/or examples of the required facts, good-faith beliefs, and/or reasons needed that would lead an officer to conclude that any type of use of force is needed. As cited with the case of the guards in Acts 27, they too, in good faith, had probable cause to believe those prisoners would escape. But a high-ranking official, [43] **...wanting to save Paul, kept [the guards] from their purpose, and commanded that those who could swim should jump overboard first and get to land, [44] and the rest, some on boards and some on parts of the ship. And so it was that they all escaped safely to land.'**

Though these prisoners could have easily swum in another direction or immediately tried to allude custody once on the island, the fact that the officers reconsidered lets us know that you, and other LEOs, could and should do the same.

Another example of an evasion can be found in Acts 16:25-28 which says,

> '...at midnight Paul and Silas were praying and singing hymns to God, and the prisoners were listening...[when] suddenly there was a great earthquake, so that the foundations of the prison were shaken; and immediately all the doors were opened, and everyone's chains were loosed. [27] And the keeper of the prison, awaking from sleep and seeing the prison doors open, supposing the prisoners had fled, drew his sword *and was about to kill himself.* [28] But Paul called with a loud voice, saying, "Do yourself no harm, for we are all here." – New King James Version

Here we find a prison guard ready to commit suicide because he thought the prisoners under his watch had fled. What would lead this guard to do such an extreme act? Again, dereliction of duty. To be seen as someone who allowed a suspect or criminal escape can be seen as such, and to that I understand. But what makes dereliction of duty different today is that Roman officers didn't have the intelligence we have today. And though there have been several technological advances, the forward thinking of law enforcement hasn't gained much traction as the same sense of duty to 'use deadly force to prevent the escape of a fleeing suspect' is often the only go-to whether 'the suspect poses a significant threat of death or serious physical injury to the officer or others' safety or not. But again, why is use-of-force the only go-to? Because again, as an officer, you *have not* done your biblical homework and *have not* made the decision to treat people as the Word instructs which means each time you're faced with split-second decisions, you'll go with your gut and respond in accordance with either your opinion or your department's position on gender and racial equality, sexual preference, the way someone looks, their national origin, age, political affiliation, financial status, religion, and/or disability. Which is why it is imperative that you get your gut in line with what God says and not what you, or others, think.

Physically Unfit to Pursue

Speaking of your gut, though I'm in no physical shape to judge but because you are in law enforcement, there is something to be said about physical fitness. When a suspect flees on foot, could it be that most officers are in no physical shape to pursue? Let's take Dallas for instance. Dallas has the 2nd largest police department in the state and is the 9th largest police force in the U.S. Yet the physical fitness portion for becoming an officer in the state requires that applicants be able to successfully complete a:

- Vertical Jump (6.5 inches)
- Bench Press, Free Weights (56% of your body weight)
- Illinois Shuttle Run (24.9 seconds)
- Sit-ups (14 in 1 minute)
- 300 Meter Run (110 seconds)
- Push-ups (4)
- 1.5 Miles Run in 19.09 minutes

With over 3,640 officers in Dallas, responsible for protecting and serving 1.34 million citizens, one has to ask, are all 3,640 in peak physical condition? Though applicants and cadets go through a rigorous physical fitness program, after taking the oath, are officers required to maintain a certain level of fitness?

I pose this question because again when you look at the officer-involved shootings, particularly of amongst African American men, who are known for their physical prowess, you have to wonder, did you shoot because you couldn't keep up or did you shoot because you were out of shape? Again, this is in no way excusing their choice to flee, but was deadly force needed? Was it a justifiable homicide because the officer gave a lawful order to stop after the suspect outran him or her or did the suspect really pose a threat? Because quite frankly that's how most officer involved shootings occur. The officer is failing horribly in his or her pursuit and with bated breath they give yet another lawful order which the suspect ignores. Because the officer did what the Fourth Amendment requires, he or she must now make a decision; to admit the fact that they are out of shape and let the suspect get away.

Of course, the obvious answer, as cited by the statistics, is to take the suspect down. But why? Again, could it be that the officer's lack of physical fitness played a role. So, the question becomes, why don't police departments require officers to always maintain peak physical condition? This is the one occupation, other than professional sports, where fitness is a priority. In fact, it is often a matter of life or death for the officer and for the public. And not only that, if the department does not require it, why doesn't the officer think it important to be in peak physical fitness; especially since his or her job is to protect the City's citizens?

A Sweet Solution

Perhaps, mandating every officer on the force, whether desk or patrol, be tested every quarter to ensure they are at their physical best. Just as applicants are required to successfully complete the physical fitness portion before they can be hired, officers should be required to maintain that same level, and exceed that requirement, depending upon tenure. If an officer fails, they should be placed on leave – without pay – until they are able to pass the fitness requirements. Why so hard? Because this is the one job where lives hang in the balance. An officer has the ability to save a life as well as take one. Anyone with that level of power should be held to a higher standard; even if it's physically. As citizens, perhaps this is something that should be taken up with our local officials.

The Wrap Up

On another note, as it pertains to evasions and Roman officers, it should be noted that Rome was known for its deplorable prisons and for their horrific treatment of both prisoners and free noncitizens alike. During those times...

> '...the Christian church would provide charity to prisoners. Emperor Constantine regulated the amount of charity the Christians could provide. A Bishop would have the right to administer [religious rites] according to Canon law. The presence of Christian priests in prisons reminded the guards to treat the prisoners well, although the prisoners still lived in horrible conditions.' [7]

And thus, as members of the body of the Lord Jesus Christ, it is still our responsibility to pray, vote, and position ourselves - as difference/decision makers – so as to remind those within the law enforcement community that according to the Sixth Amendment, every person is entitled to, 'the right of a speedy and public trial, by an impartial'[8] judge and/or jury of their peers and such sentences of death will no longer be acceptable and/or tolerated. And to be clear, we don't condone evading arrest. But it's important that we pray, vote, and position ourselves accordingly so as to prevent another Daunte, Andrew, or George from happening today.

Prayer for Citizens

Pray this with me: Heavenly Father, please give law enforcement the wherewithal to consider the value of a person's life as opposed to maiming and/or killing that person while they try to escape. Lord, I am not condoning that act, I only ask that if at all possible, and if that person poses no grave danger, that law enforcement would use their investigative skills to apprehend all suspects. Please teach them how to reassess the situation so that lives can be saved. In Jesus' name.

Prayer For Law Enforcement

Pray this with me: Heavenly Father, please forgive me for the times I used deadly and/or any kind of excessive force to prevent a suspect from fleeing. Please forgive me when I didn't consider my options. Please teach me how to de-escalate and consider other options while at the same time helping me to honor the sanctity of life, ensure there are no civilian casualties, protect those I've sworn to protect and to serve, and help me to walk away safely. In Jesus' name.

It should also be noted that a similar act occurred in Matthew 28:11-15 which says,

> **11 ... behold, some of the guard came into the city and reported to the chief priests all the things that had happened. 12 When they had assembled with the elders and consulted together, they gave a large sum of money to the soldiers [guards, officers], 13 saying, "Tell them, 'His disciples came at night and stole Him away while we slept.' 14 And if this comes to the governor's ears, we will appease him and make you secure." 15 So they took the money and did as they were instructed; and this saying is commonly reported among the Jews until this day.**

Though similar in nature, instead of contemplating suicide, the officers here took a bribe instead and were assured that the Roman governor would never know of their dereliction of duty to faithfully and honestly uphold the oath in which they swore. Whether killing someone in attempt to stop them from fleeing, committing suicide, or taking a bribe, all of the aforementioned should never be an option in the lives of integral law enforcement personnel.

And so that we know that are our prayers are not in vain, when you study the New Testament, you'll find several examples of God touching the hearts and doing a work within the Roman army (i.e., within law enforcement).

One example can be found at the crucifixion of Jesus, in Matthew 27:50-54 which reads, '**And Jesus cried out again with a loud voice, and yielded up His spirit. 51 Then, behold, the veil of the temple was torn in** two from top to bottom; and the earth quaked, and the rocks were split, ⁵² and the graves were opened; and many bodies of the saints who had fallen asleep were raised; ⁵³ and coming out of the graves after His resurrection, they went into the holy city and appeared to many. ⁵⁴ So when the centurion and those with him, who were guarding Jesus, saw the earthquake and the things that had happened, they feared greatly, saying, "Truly this was the Son of God!"** Did you notice that a Roman centurion, which would be equivalent to a lieutenant or captain today, was present when **the veil of the temple was torn in two from top to bottom; and the earth quaked, and the rocks were split, and the graves were opened; and many bodies of the saints who had fallen asleep were raised.** This Roman law enforcement agent saw the supernatural power of God – firsthand - and even went so far as to confess Jesus as Lord.

Another example of God doing a work within the Roman army or proving Himself to officers from other religions can be found in Matthew 28:4, 11-15. After Jesus' crucifixion '**...Mary Magdalene and the other Mary came to see the tomb. ² And...there was a great earthquake; for an angel of the Lord descended from heaven, and came and rolled back the stone from the door, and sat on it. ³ His countenance was like lightning, and his clothing as white as snow. ⁴ And the guards shook for fear of him, and became like dead men.'** The guards were Roman and had known Jesus had been buried. Therefore, they were present when Mary Magdalene encountered the angels and saw for themselves that the Lord's body was no longer there.

In Acts 12 we also find that Roman guards were present during Peter's incarceration as two officers were charged with guarding him, only to find him gone the next morning, after having been supernaturally released by an angel of God. Word had to have spread amongst the Roman army about the Christians because in the same chapter it says, '**Then, as soon as it was day, there was no small stir among the [Roman] soldiers about what had become of Peter.'** (v. 18) No small stir means that each time God did something amongst His people – in the presence of Rome's army – He was also simultaneously drawing Roman officers into the kingdom of God. Again, God was doing a work within the law enforcement community which lets us know – as believers He can and will do the same today when it comes to those who keep the code of silence, those who justify probable cause, those who abuse power, those who repeated give unlawful orders, and for those who exact on sight street justice. Remember when I mentioned Mr. King who stated that…

…many mistakenly believe that the Criminal Justice System is one system but, "…it's not one system, with one set of rules, or one set of laws. [It's] 30,000 microsystems; [each] with their own set of rules and policies…that… have to be changed, independently, from the inside, out."

The fact that God was doing the supernatural – in the presence of Roman officers – lets us know that God, through Mr. King, and people like you and I, can pray for Him to do the same in all 30,000 microsystems. If He did it for Rome, He can – and is – doing a work in police departments nationwide.

Something to think about...

In Fareed Zakaria's June 14, 2020, episode of Global Public Square (GPS) [9], he posed the question: What makes America's policing so different from its counterparts in the world? And what is the reason that makes America's shootings so fundamentally different than Europe?"

Paul Hirschfield, Sociology Professor at Rutgers University response:

Three main reasons. America's police as far more likely to encounter civilians in possession of firearms and so much of their training is oriented towards preventing or the scenario in their training is to respond preemptively. Unfortunately, that can result in tragic overreactions. Second of all, the threshold in which police are permitted to use deadly force and other deadly tactics in this country is much lower than the threshold in Europe (and other countries). In the United States they're permitted to use deadly force when they have a 'reasonable belief' that their life is in danger whereas in Europe that have to have an absolute necessity met. American state department legislators are free to set higher thresholds, but they rarely do so. Finally, American police receive on average about 20 weeks or five months of classroom training which is much lower than the European standard of at least two years. So, in twenty-one weeks they spend that time on essentials; the laws, rules, tactics, equipment, force, defensive techniques. Whereas in Europe they have much more time to provide a much more balanced type of educational skills programming such as cultural awareness, communications, working with a variety of groups, and a variety of tactics that will help them resolve volatile situations more peacefully."

SOURCES

1-Staff, Washington Post. "Police Shootings Database 2015-2022: Search by Race, Age, Department." *The Washington Post*, WP Company, 5 Dec. 2022.

2 - Wikipedia contributors. "Google Maps." *Wikipedia, The Free Encyclopedia*. Wikipedia, The Free Encyclopedia, 24 Jun. 2022. Web. 6 Jul. 2022.

3 Fernando, Christine. "Family of Andrew Brown Jr. Files $30M Federal Lawsuit against Deputies in Fatal Shooting." *USA Today*, Gannett Satellite Information Network, 14 July 2021.

4 - Wikipedia contributors. "George Floyd." *Wikipedia, The Free Encyclopedia*. Wikipedia, The Free Encyclopedia, 29 Nov. 2022. Web. 4 Dec. 2022.

5, 7- Wikipedia contributors. "Prisons in ancient Rome." *Wikipedia, The Free Encyclopedia*. Wikipedia, The Free Encyclopedia, 14 July 2021. Web. 4 Dec. 2022.

6 - "Fourth Amendment." *Legal Information Institute*, Cornell Legal Information Institute.

8 - "U.S. Constitution - Sixth Amendment | Resources - Congress." *Congress.gov*.

9- Fareed Zakaria GPS. Created by Fareed Zakaria, Season 2020, CNN, 14 June 2020.

Prayers of Protection and Policing Confessions for Law Enforcement

Body Armor

"Today I will be protected because I have on the whole armor of God." (Eph 6:11)

"I thank You that Your armor protects me spirit, soul, and body." (Eph 6:11)

Waist Armor

"I am placing my service weapon in my truth holster. I will operate and use it in truth.' (Eph 6:13)

Bulletproof Breastplate of Righteousness

"Though I have a bulletproof vest, I put on the breastplate of righteousness today." (Eph. 6:14)

Peacekeeping Foot Gear

"I put on my peacekeeping footgear." (Eph 6:14)

"I will be peaceful with every person I interact with today." (Eph 6:14)

"I will go into every interaction with a genuine desire to de-escalate the situation and look for see if any peaceful alternatives are available." - (Eph 6:14)

"I am an officer of peace. My Lord and Savior is the Prince of Peace. And I excel when it comes to peaceful resolutions." (Eph 6:14)

Shield of Faith

'...above all, taking the shield of faith with which you will be able to quench all the fiery darts of the wicked one.'

"I put on my shield of faith." (Eph 6:14)

"Thank You that the shield of faith protects my entire body."
(Eph 6:14)

"Though I have on tactical gear, this shield will quench all the fiery darts and serve as my backup to ensure that nothing penetrates."
(Eph 6:14)

"Thank You that the light of Your favor is shining upon my ways and surrounding me as a shield."
(Job 22:28, Psalm 5:12)

Helmet of Salvation

"I put on the helmet of salvation." (Eph 6:17)

Because I am Your child, I know that if need be You will rescue, deliver, and defend me.

"I have no doubt that I am always safe."

Service Weapon of the Spirit

"Thank You for my spiritual service weapon."

"Though I have a service weapon, I know that Your Word is sharper than any two-edged sword, piercing even to the division of soul and spirit, and of joints and marrow, and is a discerner of the thoughts and intents of the heart and will help me do my job today." (Hebrews 4:12)

"Lord, I thank You that Your Word has the ability to outperform any danger, weapon, sharp- shooter, and/or sniper on the planet."

"Not only does Your Word 'discern…the thoughts and intents of the heart,' but I thank You that whether during an interrogation or on a stop, it will decipher every code and discern every untruth for me." (Heb 4:12)

Community

"Heavenly Father, I pray for those in my department and within your community today and ask that You'd keep them away from harm and crime. I thank You for every person that I get to serve and protect. In Jesus' name."

Confidence

"I shall live and not die, and I am confident that I am doing God works shall be done while I'm on duty."
(Psalm 118:17)

Direction

"When I try to go somewhere, and the Holy Spirit does not permit be, I won't go." (Acts 16:7)

"Thank You for ordering my steps and keeping me safe." (Psalm 37:23)

Entrapment

"Thank You for keeping me from the snares that come with this job. I thank You for allowing those who set them to fall into their own nets while I escape safely. (Ps 141:9,10)

Fear

"I am strong and very courageous because I stay in the Word." (Josh 1:6)

"God has not given me the spirit of fear, but the spirit of power, love, and a sound mind." (2 Tim. 1:7)

Interactions

"I will provide soft answers to those I serve and won't respond harshly." (Pro. 15:1)

Proverbs 15:1 says, '**a soft answer turns away wrath, but a harsh word stirs up anger**.'

Justice

"Heavenly Father, just like Solomon asked for wisdom to govern,
I ask You for wisdom to administer justice." (1 Kings 3:11)

"The wisdom of God in me and I will administer justice to my community."
(1 Kings 3:28)

Objective Reasoning

"Thank You for anointing my eyes to see You as Father God." (John 17)

"Thank You that while I look at a person's outward appearance, I thank
You for teaching me how to looks at their heart." (1 Sam 16:7)

'I thank You Heavenly Father that I listen to the facts before
making a decision.' (Pro 18:3)

"I thank You that I have peace, the soul harmony which comes from
Christ ruling and acting as umpire continually in my heart while I'm on
duty and I allow Your peace to decide and settle with finality all questions
[about any subject, suspect, or situation] that [may] arise in my mind."
(Colossians 3:15)

Protection

"When it comes to policing, I am circumspect, intelligent, and wise."
(Joshua 1:6-8)

Should You tarry, I will die in a good old age, full of days, riches, and honor. (2 Chr 29:28)

The law of the Spirit of life in Christ Jesus has made me free from the law of sin and death. (Romans 8:2)

Today I will be cautious and will have the wisdom I need wherever I go.
(Joshua 1:6-8)

"Heavenly Father, thank You for traveling mercies and protection from acts of hate, injustice, and dangerous activities." (Luke 10:19)

'**[The Spirit of truth]** is guiding me into all truth **[surrounding every scene, situation, and case]**; for He will not speak on His own authority, but whatever **[The Spirit of truth]** hears **[from heaven]** He will speak [and I will hear]; and He will tell me **what I need know and do in order to be secure while protecting others.**'
(John 16:13)

"I believe in Your ability to protect me."

Strength

"I am strong in the Lord and in the power of His might.' (Ephesians 6:10)

Wisdom

Heavenly Father, I thank You for the wisdom I need today to protect and to serve. (1 Kings 3:11)

Systemic Change Prayers and Confessions for We, the People

Police Misconduct

Heavenly Father, I thank You that our police department no longer intimidates, falsely accuses its citizens, and that officers are content with their salary and benefits. (Lk. 3:14)

Heavenly Father, I ask that You'd purify the motives of law enforcement. I ask that You create in them a clean heart and renew a right, steadfast spirit within them. In Jesus' name. (Ps. 51)

Lord, I thank You for lawyers like Zenas that are leading the way in both prison and police reform. (Titus 3:13)

Heavenly Father, I ask that You help those in law enforcement to receive the instruction of wisdom, justice, judgment, and equity. (Pro 1:3) And thank You for giving them the spirit of wisdom and revelation in the knowledge of You so that they can. (Eph. 1:17)

I thank You that our police department administers justice, uses godly judgment, and are equitable when they enforce the laws and as they protect, and serve. (Pro. 1:3)

Heavenly Father, I thank You that each time law enforcement puts on their uniform, I thank You that they'll also put on tender mercies, kindness, humility, meekness, longsuffering, and love. (Col. 3:12,14)

Lord, I thank You that officer will bear with citizens and forgive the public when they go out on calls to handle complaints as You remind them that You do the same for them. (Col. 3:13)

Jails & Prisons

Heavenly Father, I thank You for prison guards and jailers like the centurion in Acts 23:17 that saved Paul's life.

I thank You for wardens, prison guards, and jailers that will protect Your children from being violated, stolen from, shanked, and killed. In Jesus' name. (Acts 23:17)

Thank You that jail and prison staff won't withhold commissary from Your children. (Acts 24:23)

I thank You for teaching probation/parole officers how to restore parolees and those on probation in the spirit of meekness. (Gal. 6:1)

Prevention of Use-of-Force

Heavenly Father, just like Julius (the centurion) kept his men from killing, I thank you for sergeants, lieutenants, captains, majors, and the like that will instruct their men to do the same. (Acts 27:42,43)

Transformation

Thank You that dishonorable law enforcement agents are becoming honorable, are being sanctified, set apart from their crooked ways and are now becoming useful, working on Your behalf, and are doing good works in their respective communities. (2 Tim. 2:20, 21)

'Heavenly Father, I thank You for raising up brilliant, integral, Holy Spirit filled, tongue-talking, Bible reading, knee praying, biblical living officers, sergeants, lieutenants, captains, majors, and the like.'

Lord, I thank You for lawyers like Zenas that are working diligently for their clients. (Titus 3:13)

Humility

"Lord, You said that the humble You guide in justice, so I thank You for humble officers. In Jesus' name."
(Psalm 25:9)

Judicial

'Thank You for judges that will judge rightly, honestly, and fearlessly like Deborah.' Judges 4:4-9

"Thank You that the citizens of our county are delivered from the influence, rule, jurisdiction, strength, and authority of wrongful, long, extended, harsh and unlawful sentences from crooked and unmerciful judges, prosecutors, investigators, experts, and lawyers influenced by the powers of darkness.' Colossians 1:12-14

'God of justice, 1 Kings 3:28 says that You gave Solomon wisdom to administer justice. Therefore, I ask You to show Judge _____ and the prosecuting lawyer how to do the same. Please give them the wisdom and understanding (he/she) needs to ensure that _____ is proven not guilty.'

'Lord, You said in Proverbs 21:1 that the king's heart is in Your hand, and You turn it wherever You wish. I pray that You would turn the hearts of the prosecutors and the judge towards justice and the truth.

Thank You for appointing merciful judges
and district attorneys.
(James 2:13)

Thank You for judges who will extend mercy during sentencing.
(James 2:13)

Justice

"Lord, it is so good to know that You love *justice*, and that You will not forsake Your saints." (Psalm 37:28)

Lord, I thank You that every morning You bring justice to light. (Zephaniah 3:5)

Lord, I thank You for those whom You created to do justice. I thank You that they are experiencing joy and that destruction is coming to the workers of lawlessness. (Proverbs 21:15)

"Thank You for electing judges and officers that will judge and administer just judgment." (Deuteronomy 16:18)

"Thank You that officers in my county won't pervert justice, show partiality, take a bribe, or twist the words of the righteous. (Deuteronomy 16:18)

"Thank You that officers in my county are learning to do good, are seeking justice, rebuking traffickers, racists, and those who would pervert the truth. I thank You they are defending the fatherless and helping orphans in their community as well as looking out for the widow." (Isaiah 1:17)

Law of the Spirit of Life in Christ Jesus

The law of the spirit of life in Christ Jesus is causing harsh sentences and sentence enhancements to be reduced nationwide. (Romans 8:2)

The law of the spirit of life in Christ Jesus is above every penal code in the land, so Lord, I thank You for stays, exonerations, and overruling death penalties. In Jesus' name.

The law of the spirit of life in Christ Jesus supersedes, overrides, and is higher than all 18,000+ penal codes, including those that the wrongly accused and convicted have been charged and/or convicted of. So, I thank You Lord for sentence reductions and/or early releases. (Rom 8:2)

Mark 11:22-24 says, "'Have faith in God. ^{23} For assuredly, [Jesus said that]...[if I say]...to this [mountainous conviction], 'Be removed [reduced, overturned], and be cast into the sea,' and don't doubt in [my] heart, but believe that [reduction, overturning, and release are possible then] those things [I] say will be done, [and I say that _____]...will have [freedom]...^{24} [And because Jesus said]...whatever things [I] ...ask [about his/her sentence] when [I] pray, [because I] believe that [I will] receive...and...will have [what I say].' (author paraphrase) Therefore, I believe and say that _____'s sentence will be reduced, commuted, and/or overturned or he/she will be paroled and/or have his/her appeal granted. In Jesus' name.

Medical Attention

Heavenly Father, thank You for guards and officers who will render aid when Your children need it. In Jesus' name. (Acts 16:33)

Just like the guard did for Paul and Silas, I thank You for personnel who give Your People immediate medical attention. In Jesus' name. (Acts 16:33)

New Officers

"Lord, I thank You for wise men who understand the times, know law and how to administer justice.' (Esther 1:13)

I thank You for truthful officers who will take their responsibility, to protect and to serve to heart. I thank You that You've raised up new officers who will execute justice for the oppressed, give food to vulnerable populations and will be merciful when given the opportunity to grant citations and warnings. In Jesus' name. (Psalm 146:6, 7)

"Thank You for removing officers who do not understand justice and replacing them with those who seek You." (Proverbs 28:5)

"Thank You for officers who won't neglect the weightier matters of the law such as justice, mercy, faith and the love of God." (Matthew 23:23)

Parole Hearings

'I thank You for qualifying _____ for a pardon, parole, and/or short-term probation because he/she is a partaker of the inheritance of freedom with the saints in the light.' (Colossians 1:12-14)

'_____ will successfully comply and complete the terms of his/her parole and/or probation and will never do anything that will cause him/her to have to return to prison.'

'Just as God did for Barabbas, he is doing for _____. His/her parole will be granted.' (Matthew 26)

Prison Staff and Treatment

'Heavenly Father, I thank You that the prison staff will no longer intimidate or falsely accuse me and other inmates and that they'll no longer extort us but will be content with their wages.' (Luke 3:14 prayer)

'Just as Julius treated Paul kindly and gave him liberty, thank You for guards treat Your children the same way.' (Acts 27:3)

'Prison guards will be changed because of how they see You work in the lives of Your children while they are incarcerated.' (Acts 16:29-34)

'God is ensuring that His children are rehabilitated and prepared for release by competent correctional staff and administrators like Julius.' (Col 1:12; Acts 27:3)

'Thank You for correctional staff, like Julius, who are ensuring Your children receive the medical assistance and care they need.' (Acts 27:3)

'Just like the guard did for Paul and Silas, I thank You for personnel who'll give Your children immediate medical attention.' (Acts 16:33)

'Thank You that, like Julius, the correctional staff are ensuring that Your children's civil liberties aren't being violated.' (Acts 27:3)

Protection

'Should the tarry Lord, I thank You that officers will die in a good old age, full of days, riches, and honor.' (1 Chr. 29:28)

'Heavenly Father, just as the two angels prevented Lot's family from being violated, I thank You for sending Your angels to prevent officers from sexually violated Your people.' (Genesis 19:1-24 prayer)

'I pray that officers put on their armor today. Their waists are girded with truth. They have on breastplates of righteousness and their feet are shod with the preparation of the gospel of peace. I thank You for giving them the shield of faith and teaching them how to use the sword of the spirit.' (Ephesians 6:14-17)

Repentance

'God of mercies, please forgive Officer _____.
I know he/she was wrong and that he/she should be punished. Lord, I understand he/she must be judged in the courts, but I ask that You'd mercifully judge him/her; so as to ensure they he/she is sentenced fairly. In Jesus' name.' (prayer)

'Heavenly Father, though _____ is in opposition to what You want for (him/her), I ask that You would grant (him/her) the gift of repentance, so that (he/she) may know the truth, and come to (his/her) senses and escape the snare of the devil (gangs, addiction, hustling, distractions, wrong people, lack of vision, ignorance, the legal system, and greed).' (2 Timothy 2:25, 26)

'Lord, I know _____ may not have asked You
To forgive him/her but I ask You to be good to that officer because it's Your goodness that will lead him/her to repentance.' (Rom 2:4)

'God, I ask that You would be good to Officer _____ and lead him/her to repent.' (Rom 2:4)

Strength

"Lord, I pray that You give officers the strength, might, and patience to long suffer with those they serve." (Colossians 1:10, 11)

'Heavenly Father, I ask You to teach officers how to pray in tongues and give them the grace needed to protect and to serve." (John 14:2)

'Heavenly Father I ask that You fill officers within my county with the ability to think, do, and believe the impossible through Your Spirit in their inner man. I pray that Christ would dwell in their hearts through faith and that You would root and ground them in Your love.
(Ephesians. 3:16, 17 prayer)

'Lord, I thank You for giving officers the help of the Holy Spirit and that He is encouraging them.' (John 14:16)

Supply of the Spirit

'Thank You Heavenly Father for giving officers a supply of the Spirit of Jesus Christ today.' (Philippians 1:19)

Appendix

Appendix 1.1: Chapter 6, 'Objective Reasoning'

Immersion Learning

A practical application of meditating is referred to as Immersion Learning. Immersion Learning is when a pupil immerses themselves, heart, mind, and body into a particular subject. Say for instance you wanted to learn Mandarin. A good way to learn would be to move to China and become totally immersed in the culture. By living amongst, working with, and interacting with the people, you'd become acclimated to the language. The same is true for your courage and your overall protection as a law enforcement agent. You can totally immerse yourself into the kingdom of God – from the comfort of your home, patrol car, and/or office - by immersing yourself in the Word of God. The best way to get started is to read, listen to, watch, and talk about NOTHING but faith and God's protection. To give you an example of how immersion works can be found with Dr. Creflo Dollar.

Immersion in Action

Dr. Creflo Dollar, Senior Pastor of World Changers Church International, once gave his testimony about doing exactly this when he was diagnosed with prostate cancer. He said the moment he received the diagnosis, he realized he was under attack. He realized this wasn't just about being sick or having some disease; but he understood that his *very existence* was at stake. He then decided to IMMERSE himself on nothing but healing teachings.

Dr. Dollar went on to share that during that time, he didn't want to *talk* about anything but healing. He didn't want to *hear* anything but healing. And he didn't want to see any programming that didn't have to do with healing. This is because he *had to* become so IMMERSED that he could speak the language of healing because remember, Proverbs 18:21 says, '**Death and life are in the power of the tongue, and those who love it will eat its fruit.**' Even though *his body* was telling him he was sick, he had to align his words so that they came into agreement with what *God's Word* said, as opposed to agreeing with the cancer that was trying to ravage his body.

> '...He was wounded for our transgressions, He was bruised for our iniquities; the chastisement for our peace was upon Him, and by [Jesus'] stripes we are healed.' Isaiah 53:5

The Word said he was healed which meant in spite of the symptoms and pain he was experiencing, he had to feed his mind and spirit with what God said. The same is true for you.

Joshua 1 says to,

> '...**be strong and very courageous, that you may observe to do according to all the law...do not turn from it to the right hand or to the left, that you may prosper wherever you go. This Book of the Law shall not depart from your mouth, but you shall meditate in it day and night...for then you will make your way prosperous...**'
> – Joshua 1:6-8

Even though fellow officers, Supervisors, and/or other personnel may, '...scorn, shun, exclude, condemn, harass, and almost invariably, cast [you] out', you have to know, beyond a shadow of a doubt, that God promised you'd prosper which again means that He'll cause you to know when to look around, be cautious, give you the street savvy and wisdom you need..."**wherever you go.**"

By immersing yourself in the Word, you are refusing fear the right to remain in your thoughts. But in order to get to the point where you're able to know-that-you-know-that-you-know-that you are protected, you must first immerse yourself on faith, angelic assistance, and instances of God's protection found throughout scripture.

You see immersion learning is much like starting a new job. On the first day, you really don't know what to expect. Though you may have experience with how to do the job, you're unfamiliar with their processes. Plus, you're unfamiliar with their policies. The same is true with God's protection. The more you immerse yourself in it, the more familiar you'll become with the policies of God. Without immersing yourself, fear will continue to speak to you and become so *loud* that you won't be able to believe that angelic protection is possible. The way to *silence* the noisiness of the fear is to listen to, watch, talk about, read, and totally saturate yourself in the Word of God UNTIL YOU ARE TOTALLY CONVINCED AND CONFIDENT THAT GOD WILL PROTECT. I repeat, the way to *silence* the noisiness of the fear and shunning is to listen to, watch, talk about, read, and totally saturate yourself UNTIL YOU ARE TOTALLY CONVINCED.

> '¹He who dwells in the secret place of the Most High shall abide under the shadow of the Almighty. ² I will say of the Lord, "He is my refuge and my fortress; my God, in Him I will trust." ³ Surely He shall deliver you from the snare of the fowler and from the perilous pestilence. ⁴ He shall cover you with His feathers, and under His wings you shall take refuge; His truth shall be your shield and buckler. ⁵ You shall not be afraid of the terror by night, nor of the arrow that flies by day, ⁶ Nor of the pestilence that walks in darkness, nor of the destruction that lays waste at noonday.'
> Ps. 91:1-6

You're going to have to make the decision that the only thing going on in your home, patrol car, and/or office is protection. Nothing more. Nothing less. You are going to have to eat, drink, and breathe protection every moment of the day until you are fully persuaded that you're making the right decision. You don't have time to watch, listen, or pay attention to anything or anyone not talking about protection because again, too much is at stake. So before we go any further, settle it in your heart that for however long it takes, you are going to eat, breathe and do nothing but immerse on protection. So, to help you get started…

Pray this with me: Heavenly Father, please help me to immerse myself in protection. I have never done anything like this before and I don't know how or where to start but Lord I am willing so that I can be a better man, officer, and more importantly, child of God. Please give me the interest, patience, and attention span needed to immerse myself until I am totally convinced of Your protection and that I am making the right decision. In Jesus' name.

And wouldn't you know it? God has already answered your prayer! Here's a few ways to help you get your immersion started.

WAYS TO IMMERSE

When you wake: Set your alarm 15 minutes earlier to pray (in the Spirit) and make your protection confessions found in the Prayers of Protection and Policing Confessions section.

Getting ready for work: Listen to faith-building protection teachings or music while showering and getting dressed.

If you take public transit: Read your Bible or listen to protection teachings on your device.

Commuting To Work: Listen to faith-building teachings. According to the U.S. Census Bureau[8], the average American spends at least 100 hours commuting to work. You can obtain an associate degree in less than 67 hours. Just think if you used this time to build yourself up in the Word.

At your workstation: Keep your protection verses in your desk drawer, as a screensaver or on your device so that you can see them every time you open it and if allowed, continue to listen to faith-based teachings or music. If your workstation is your patrol car, even better.

On your break: Take a prayer walk or go to your car for those 15 minutes and just be quiet.

Social Media: The time spent checking social media, devote to immersing.

On your lunch: Read your Bible, take another prayer walk, or listen to teachings in your patrol car. Get with another believing officer and just fellowship. Or make more protection confessions over yourself to ensure the rest of your shift goes well.

While you're in the grocery store, gym, or at your child's practice: Put on your earbuds and listen to teachings.

After you get home from work: Instead of reaching for the remote, take a moment to pray, watch BVOV.tv or other protective teachings or simply be quiet.

In your kitchen: Keep a scripture God has put on your heart on the refrigerator door and say it out loud while preparing your meals.

While you're preparing your meals: Put your laptop in the kitchen and download some teachings. While you're cooking, ask your child to confess a few of their protection scriptures.

While you're cleaning the house: Turn up with worship music.

In your bathroom: Have a faith-building protection book readily available.

When you lay down: Download a faith teaching or listen to a Bible app and allow the Word of God to feed you while you sleep.

Go to bed: At least twenty minutes earlier and read the Word out loud. You don't have to read several chapters, but at least one a day or write in your Companion Journal about what the Lord did for you that day.

Pray and just be still: Do this without any television or music going. And everyone can do this one...

With all that being said, you may have to make your confessions daily for several weeks or even months before your faith is truly built up to the point that you know that you know that you know that you're convinced and ready. But please know, this is not a formula. This is *you* using the measure of faith God has given *you* to receive the protection Christ died to ensure and God promised you'd have.

Appendix 1.2: Chapter 12: Psychological Evaluations

A Sweet Solution: The Corrective Accountability Act

After watching a session about the Justice System and Rehabilitation with Reginald Dwayne Betts, Marcia Chatlain and Marc Howard on CSPAN® in January 2018, I was more determined than ever to pray about the great points each made about prison reform. One of which was rehabilitation and the corrective aspect. I saw that there has to be some type of corrective accountability, not just for the inmates, but for the staff. In that since prisons are commonly referred to as the Department of Corrections, there has to be a way to monitor and incentivize staff performance, as it pertains to correction.

A way to do it would be to create a performance-based system that holds staff accountable for inmate rehabilitation throughout their sentence. Again, since it is called the Department of Corrections, they should be accountable *and incentivized* for the positive corrections they attribute to. But it wasn't until I was reading an article about U. Renee Hall, Dallas' first female police chief, that I began to see the importance of this type of incentive. This type of incentive needs to occur on the municipal level first before it makes its way elsewhere.

With police officers wanting higher pay, they should be able to earn it based not only upon their ability *to protect,* but also *to serve.* Whereas before, performance was based on crime levels i.e., their ability to protect, it should also include what they're doing in their respective communities. Since each officer is assigned to a precinct, within each precinct there could be a citizens' review board that conducts quarterly and/or annual reviews of what the community thinks of each officer. Anonymous feedback and surveys could be provided by mail, in person, or online as to what each citizen thinks about that officer's performance. If the officer has no reviews or feedback, therein lies the problem. They have no engagement with the community and thus would determine a portion of their annual performance review for salary increases. If an officer has formal complaints, that would be taken into consideration, and if an officer has criminal charges pending, that would be taken into account as well. Both would be separate from the citizens' review board.

Who would serve on the citizens' review board? Those whom the community selects, delegated organizations, and/or individuals who submits an application of interest. Both would be reviewed by the police departments, but neither would be selected by the police department.

How would an officer serve? They would each (as in EVERY OFFICER) be required to submit a *Service Proposal* after a period of time of what they think is needed in a particular neighborhood. Within the Service Proposal would be low-cost ways to meet those needs which would be approved by the chief of police and/or department heads. If approved, the officer would then be responsible for obtaining that particular neighborhood's buy-in. And herein is where community engagement comes into play.

Former Dallas Police Chief Renee Hall stated in her interview with Jaime Thompson of D Magazine that majors and chiefs, '...*needed to get closer to their troops.*' She said that '*she'd heard from officers that they rarely saw majors and chiefs around their precincts, and that was unacceptable.*' She then made it a requirement that they both, '...*know the police officers up under [their] command*' because they were, '...*making decisions that affected them each and every day, and how [could they] do that if [they] didn't...know who [they were] making decisions for?"* The same is true for officers. How can they serve a community that they've only resigned themselves to protect? By paying attention, interacting, and being proactive about solving problems that plague their respective communities, this would allow them to SERVE those communities. But let's take it a step further. Once their *Service Proposals* were approved, each would be responsible for hiring citizens - within those neighborhoods - to do the work within the community.

What needs to be included in the Service Proposal?

- An identifiable problem within a particular community and/or specific neighborhood
- Crime rates
- Racial demographics
- Economic demographics
- An actionable solution to the problem
- A service for the solution (i.e., Why funding is needed)
- Low-cost ways to fund the solution would include a list of at least one potential local, state, and/or federal grants, private donor and/or corporate sponsor.

- Turn-around time for the solution (i.e., How long will it take to get off the ground, gain community support and outcomes?)
- Citizen Review Board (i.e., Recommendations of whom they think should serve on the board. Must include at least three letters of recommendations from those active in the community which may include neighborhood watches and associations)

How would the Service Proposals be funded? Local, state, and federal grants. Also, by private donations and corporate sponsors. All of which would be the officer's duty to canvas and locate.

How does this tie into performance? The success of the service determines 50% of the officer's increase (50% protection performance – 50% service performance). Success Reviews would occur quarterly but compensated annually. The rate of success and/or increase would be determined by police leadership.

Outcomes - The goal of Correctional Accountability is to provide a way for local, state, and federal officers to play a more active role in corrections, both inside and outside of prison. The way to prevent long-term corrections is to correct behaviors within the community before it starts. By creating a service-based means for officers to be compensated for correcting i.e., serving their respective communities by course correcting their community's byway of creating jobs and opportunities for citizens to earn income that ordinarily would have been obtained by committing a crime, is the best and safest alternative.

By doing so, the entire process will allow the officer to become sensitive to serving the people within the community as opposed to just protecting and punishing them. The process will also endear him or her to their community, and vice versa...as was the case for Cornelius.

Statewide and Federal Level - On a broader note, as it pertains to correctional facilities, the aforementioned can be done on an individual scale with an added bonus for anti-recidivism which would ensure successful re-entry. The system has to address the roles and responsibilities and while providing a metric in the time that it has to be done, which should be determined by the earliest possible release date or should flow in conjunction to appeals. The goal is to ensure that the staff not only oversees and supervises the day-to-day activities of inmates, but also ensure their success while in custody *and beyond*.

Though this is just an idea, I'd like to ask you to prayerfully consider. Prayerfully, it can become a bill entitled the Corrective Accountability Act.

SOURCES

Wikipedia contributors. "Probable cause." *Wikipedia, The Free Encyclopedia*. Wikipedia, The Free Encyclopedia, 27 May. 2022. Web. 18 Jun. 2022.

Wikipedia contributors. "Failure to obey a police order." *Wikipedia, The Free Encyclopedia*. Wikipedia, The Free Encyclopedia, 3 Dec. 2022. Web. 4 Dec. 2022.

Wikipedia contributors. "Title 18 of the United States Code." *Wikipedia, The Free Encyclopedia*. Wikipedia, The Free Encyclopedia, 31 Oct. 2022. Web. 4 Dec. 2022.

"Welcome to NYC.gov | City of New York." *The Official Website of the City of New York*, City of New York,

Wikipedia contributors. "Centurion." *Wikipedia, The Free Encyclopedia*. Wikipedia, The Free Encyclopedia, 2 Jun. 2022. Web. 11 Jun. 2022.

Dallas, Texas Population 2022, http://worldpopulationreview.com/us-cities/dallas-population/.

Thompson, Jamie. "This Is the New Chief of Police." *D Magazine*, 14 June 2019.

If you'd like to **purchase bulk copies** or your organization needs a **Guest Podcast/Speaker, Commentator or Panelist** about law enforcement issues in the Bible, please email **info@stacisweet.com** or visit my website at **stacisweet.com**.

Other Works

Policing in Faith Companion Journal

Crime, Criminals & Redemption: What the Bible Says About Crime and Those Who Commit Them

Crime, Criminals, and Redemption: A Companion Confessional for Loved Ones

The Elephant in the Room: Hard Conversations About Faith and Race

The New 'It': 11 Whole Weeks of Nothing But It

Deep-Pression: Toggling Between the Worlds of Mental Illness and Hyper Spirituality

The Do-It-Yourself Guide out of Homelessness: A Call-To-Action Guide Written For the Homeless

INDEX

Civilian Complaint Process, 23-25, 27

Closing the Law Enforcement Consent Loophole Act, 62, 82, 137

Code of Silence, 27-37, 40, 45, 46, 71, 104, 117, 153, 177

Correction, 39-60, 209-212

Deadly Force, 79, 80, 89-92, 97-102, 113, 114, 146, 148, 149, 159, 167-173, 178

Defund the Police Movement, 41, 113, 163-165

Dereliction of Duty, 19, 20, 169-178

Escapes, 19-21, 90-92, 157, 167-178

Evasions, 19-21, 90-92, 157, 167-178

Fourth Amendment, 88-92, 170, 171, 173

Good Cops, 151-158

Graham v. Connor, 69-74, 77-93

Lawful Orders, 77-93, 115, 176, 177

Objective Reasoning, 61-74, 91-93, 97-110, 112, 161, 168

Officer Suicides, 17-21, 171, 175-178

Police Brutality, 7, 15, 17, 41, 102, 145-149

Posthumous Exonerations, 15, 34-37

Probable Cause, 77-93, 99, 102, 170, 171

Psychological Evaluations, 159-162

Repentance, 39-60

Serious Bodily Injury, 80, 101, 102, 113, 134, 146-149

Soft Use-of-Force, 145, 146

Tennessee v. Garner, 77-93, 90-92, 170-172

Use of Force, 41, 48, 67, 72, 77-93, 145-149

Use-of-Force in the Bible, 145-149

www.ingramcontent.com/pod-product-compliance
Lightning Source LLC
Chambersburg PA
CBHW060947050426
42337CB00052B/1636